Contents

Authors

Jody Hoff is the vice-president and program administrator for the Idaho Council on Economic Education in Boise, Idaho. Her responsibilities include program development, delivery, and evaluation. She holds teaching certificates in Economics, Mathematics, and Social Studies. Prior to her work with the Idaho Council, Jody taught math and economics in Idaho public schools. She began her work in curriculum development with PBS, developing classroom lessons and activities in the area of mathematics and technology. Jody is an advocate of the active learning model, incorporating creative "experiences" into classroom lessons and activities. She has been awarded teaching honors from the University of Idaho, the Idaho Council on Economic Education, the National Teacher Training Institute, and National Association of Economic Educators.

Sarapage McCorkle is the director of the Center for Entrepreneurship and Economic Education at the University of Missouri-St. Louis. Dr. McCorkle has taught economics for 31 years at the university. She has written an economics textbook for K-8 teachers and over 17 economic education curriculum units that focus on teaching economics, personal finance, and entrepreneurship. She has twice received the Leavey Award for Excellence in Private Enterprise Education and two national awards in economic education. In recent years, Dr. McCorkle has taught economic education to educators from countries of the Baltics, central and eastern Europe, and the former Soviet Union.

Mary Suiter is the associate director of the Center for Entrepreneurship and Economic Education at the University of Missouri-St. Louis. Ms. Suiter served on the 10-member writing team for K-12 national economics standards. Suiter has authored/co-authored numerous lessons and curriculum units that are used nationally and internationally to teach economics in the K-12 classroom. These include *Zooconomy: Zoo Business*, *Arts Mart*, *Economics and Children's Literature*, *The Voyages of Columbus: An Economic Enterprise*, *Kaleidoscope USA*, *The Economics of Our Diverse Society*, and *Economics: Focus Middle School*, *Financial Fitness for Life: Steps to Financial Fitness* and *Money Math: Lessons for Life*. Suiter developed stories and lessons for Wise Pockets World, a web site for young children. She has conducted economic education workshops nationally and internationally.

James Bettendorf is a veteran mathematics educator who has worked for over 30 years in Minnesota's St. Cloud Area School District. He has served on the district's staff development team as well as Minnesota's Best Practices Network, a teacher association for sharing exemplary teaching resources and expertise, and St. Cloud State University. Mr. Bettendorf also worked as a specialist for the state's Department of Children, Families and Learning. He is currently retired but continues to work part time at the department.

Lisa Breidenbach teaches mathematics at Tecumseh Middle School, Lafayette, Indiana. Ms. Breidenbach's varied experience includes teaching sixth through twelfth grade mathematics, writing curriculum materials, organizing and conducting professional development experiences, and speaking at teacher conferences from the local to national levels.

Pamela Cornwell has taught middle school math at Pattonville School District in St. Louis, MO for 12 years. She also serves as an adjunct for the University of Missouri - St. Louis and teaches math methods courses for elementary, middle school, and special education majors.

Acknowledgments

The members of the writing team express their deepest gratitude to the many individuals who were involved with this project.

Reviewers:

Economics Educators:

Peter Moore, Director
Center for Economic Education
Rhode Island College
Providence, RI

Helen Roberts, Associate Director
University of Illinois at Chicago
Chicago, IL

Mathematics Educators:

Jean Brown, Sixth Grade Mathematics Teacher
Wright Elementary School, Chicago, IL

Carlos Borges, Seventh Grade Mathematics Teacher
Chase Elementary School, Chicago, IL

Judy DeJan, Curriculum Coordinator
Chase Elementary School, Chicago, IL

Jason Dzijia, Seventh Grade Mathematics Teacher
Chase Elementary School, Chicago, IL

Emily Johns, Eighth Grade Mathematics Teacher
Chase Elementary School, Chicago, IL

Patti Kushner, Seventh Grade Mathematics Teacher
Chase Elementary School, Chicago, IL

Maldon Mallett, Eighth Grade Mathematics Teacher
Wright Elementary School, Chicago, IL

Eric Runyan, Fifth Grade Mathematics Teacher
Chase Elementary School, Chicago, IL

Bradley Stone, Eighth Grade Mathematics Teacher
Chase Elementary School, Chicago, IL

Foreword

This excellent book is aptly named. Bringing mathematics and economics together–connecting them effectively in the minds of our students–will give those young people very important skills they can use in their lives, all their lives.

For more than 50 years, the National Council on Economic Education (NCEE) has been the nation's leader in getting economics into the K–12 curriculum of the nation's schools by teaching teachers and equipping them with outstanding materials.

This publication, however, is part of an exciting new series of publications for NCEE. It is especially written for middle school mathematics teachers. It will have significant reach and impact, in terms of core educational experiences for thousands of young people. We are very grateful to 3M for making this splendid resource for teachers possible. NCEE is proud of this outstanding partnership with 3M–and of the product.

Because understanding economics is so important for success in life, NCEE is constantly seeking ways to ensure that economics is incorporated into teaching and learning in various subject areas, especially the social studies, such as government, history, geography, and now mathematics. This new teaching resource will certainly help to advance economic literacy, because of the central place math has in the curriculum in all schools.

Whether the course is a sixth grade general mathematics class or an eighth grade pre-Algebra class, there are lessons here designed to help reinforce the mathematics concepts and processes taught, by using examples from economics. Using the four basic mathematical manipulations of addition, subtraction, multiplication, and division, students will understand how to construct a price index to compare the costs of goods and wages today with those in the past. They also compare the costs of goods in different countries by looking at exchange rates. Students also learn the basics of supply and demand and how the equilibrium price of a good is determined. This book is especially designed to help mathematics teachers answer the proverbial question asked by students, "Why do I have to learn this? Am I ever going to use it?"

On the other hand, mathematics teachers may ask the question, "Do I need to take a course in economics in order to use this curriculum guide?" The answer is, "No." This book was specifically written for mathematics educators, in consultation with mathematics educators. It provides the needed economics, as well as the answers to problems/questions. However, if you or your students have questions to which you do not know the economics answer, please visit our website www.ncee.net to find the nearest NCEE Council or Center Director–who can certainly help you.

The primary authors of this work, outstanding economic educators, Jody Hoff, Sarapage McCorkle, and Mary Suiter, consulted with three excellent mathematics educators, James Bettendorf, Lisa Breidenbach, and Pamela Cornwell, and we are most grateful to them. Special thanks also go to John Clow, Director of the Leatherstocking Center for Economic Education in Oneonta, New York, for his work in getting this project launched, and to Elizabeth Volard, former Senior Vice President at NCEE, for her vision for developing curriculum materials for mathematics teachers that reinforce mathematics concepts using examples from economics. NCEE is especially appreciative of the exceptional partnership with the National Council of Teachers of Mathematics (NCTM), which, with the support of 3M, truly made this good work possible.

Robert F. Duvall, Ph.D.
President & Chief Executive Officer
The National Council on Economic Education

Introduction

Mathematics and Economics: Connections for Life, 6-8 is a set of 12 lessons that demonstrate how mathematical processes and concepts may be applied to the study of economics and personal finance. In this volume, mathematics educators will find lessons connecting mathematics instruction to practical problems and issues that students will encounter throughout their lifetimes.

In the study of these problems and issues, economics and mathematics are natural intellectual allies. Economics is the study of people's attempts to make good decisions in an uncertain world endowed with limited resources. The tools that economists use gain power, elegance and visual appeal as they are represented mathematically in models. Indeed, one might think of economics as "first quadrant math" because economic magnitudes only rarely take on a negative sign. Research indicates that students with a strong background in mathematics are more likely than others to succeed in introductory college-level economics classes. However, the lessons presented here are not designed solely for use with students who are college-bound. These lessons are designed to provide economic skills and knowledge that all students will use as savers, investors, consumers, producers, and informed citizens.

Using the Lessons

The minimum level of mathematics students must have for each lesson is noted in the Mathematics Focus section of each lesson. Each lesson begins with a mathematical warm-up activity to introduce the mathematics content of the economics lesson. Activity sheets, answers, visuals for making overhead transparencies and extension activities are provided in each lesson, ready to be copied for use. Each lesson also includes a detailed lesson procedure section with background on the concepts being taught.

These lessons are NOT intended for use in teaching mathematics processes and concepts; rather, they illustrate economic and personal finance applications for the mathematics knowledge and skills students have already acquired in their mathematics classes. As a result, these lessons are well suited for use as culminating activities in mathematics courses, or they may be used between units to offer a change of pace and a meaningful application of mathematics to a real-world problem.

Overview of the Lessons

In Lesson 1 of this volume, students use currency exchange rates to convert the prices of a Big Mac™ in different countries into U. S. dollars. They determine in which country a Big Mac™ is cheapest and most expensive in terms of U. S. dollars. Finally, students calculate the percentage of daily income (per capita GDP per day) that is required in each country to purchase a Big Mac™ in terms of the local currency. In Lesson 2, students continue to learn about exchange rates as they listen to the story of an American girl who is planning a trip to Mexico. In this lesson, they compare exchange rates to determine if one currency has appreciated or depreciated against another currency. They analyze how changes in exchange rates affect the prices of goods and services from another country.

In Lesson 3, students analyze data for baby-sitting wages (a price for labor) and the price of movie tickets since 1945. This lesson provides the foundation for lessons on inflation and its impact on purchasing power over time. Lesson 4 introduces students to the Consumer Price Index and the construction of price indexes. They learn how a price index is used to compare incomes and prices from year to year.

Lesson 5 is designed to introduce students to the benefits of competition utilizing proportions to compare different rates. Students will explore the market for cell phones in two activities. In Activity 1, students are asked to solve for the unit rate of several cell phone providers and draw conclusions about the relative costs. In Activity 2, students take on the role of a cell phone service provider and put together a monthly plan to sell to customers. The lesson concludes with students graphing the unit rates for cell phone airtime over several periods and summarizing their findings.

Lesson 6 is designed to reinforce the usefulness of percentages in comparing fractions of unequal size and provide students with practice in using percent to calculate simple interest. Students are introduced to the idea of buying on credit and the additional resources required to service the debt. The concept of costs and benefits will be examined as students compare the additional cost of borrowing money to purchase the bike with the additional benefits of having the bike right now.

Lesson 7 focuses on a topic that is at the heart of economics, that of decision-making. Decision-making from an economic perspective requires individuals to consider both the benefits and costs for each alternative. Human nature however often makes this benefit-cost analysis a forgone conclusion as people emphasize the benefits of what they think they want and ignore or minimize the costs of what they think is the less attractive alternative. Students will apply several important mathematics skills in the process of learning about economic decision-making. In Activity 1, student teams develop selection factors and a weighting scheme to select a particular type of pet. In Activity 2, student teams are given scenarios and are asked to make a pet decision. Student teams will then present their decision solution to the class.

Lesson 8 is designed to acquaint students with the relationship between earnings and education. The data is very clear regarding one's earning potential and educational attainment, that is, the more education an individual has the greater his or her earning potential. This is an important life lesson for students to explore as they begin forming opinions about the value of school and their own education. Students will utilize their mathematics skills to explore the relationship between earnings and education. The economics involved in the lesson will require students to define earnings and human capital.

Lesson 9 introduces students to the idea that not all skills are valued equally in the marketplace. The students will explore these differences using their mathematics skills to create box and whisker plots. Students will generate their own data on the value of skills by using a bidding activity. Students are given a budget and instructed to purchase the skills needed to survive on a deserted island.

Lessons 10 and 11 focus on identifying where prices come from. In Lesson 10 students will complete a series of activities that represent supply and demand. In the first activity, students are asked to plot points, connect the points through a straight line, and write the equation for the line. The two sets of data represent supply and demand for pizza in the small town of Pizzaville. In Activity 2, students compare and contrast the two linear equations. Finally in the third activity, students combine the supply and demand curves to find the intersection point and identify that point as the market price. The formal terms of supply, demand, and equilibrium are introduced. In Lesson 11 students continue to examine where prices come from, as students apply the concepts of supply, demand, and equilibrium. Students will examine changes within a market for pizza utilizing linear equations as the vehicle for examining shifting supply and demand equations. Transformation of linear equations and calculating the new intersection will provide students with the framework for exploring the dynamics of a market. In Lesson 12 students learn what a budget is. They construct a pie chart to show the distribution of expenses in a budget. They learn about payroll deductions and determine the impact that payroll deductions have on a budget. Finally, they learn that the U.S. federal government uses tax revenue to pay for the goods and services it uses and provides. They construct graphs that represent the federal government's budget of projected income and expenses for 2002.

Correlation of *Mathematics and Economics: Connections for Life* Lessons with the National Standards for Mathematics

Mathematics Standards	Lesson 1	Lesson 2	Lesson 3	Lesson 4	Lesson 5	Lesson 6	Lesson 7	Lesson 8	Lesson 9	Lesson 10	Lesson 11	Lesson 12
1. Number and Operations	X	X		X	X	X	X	X				X
2. Algebra	X			X						X	X	
3. Geometry												
4. Measurement												
5. Data Analysis & Probability			X					X	X			X
6. Problem Solving							X					X
7. Reasoning and Proof												
8. Communication							X					X
9. Connections												X
10. Representation												

Correlation of *Mathematics and Economics: Connections for Life* Lessons with the National Standards for Economics

Economic Standards	Lesson 1	Lesson 2	Lesson 3	Lesson 4	Lesson 5	Lesson 6	Lesson 7	Lesson 8	Lesson 9	Lesson 10	Lesson 11	Lesson 12
1. Scarcity												
2. Marginal costs/marginal benefits						X	X					
3. Allocation of goods and services												
4. Role of incentives												
5. Gain from trade												
6. Specialization and trade												
7. Markets – price and quantity determination	X	X								X		
8. Role of price in market system												
9. Role of competition					X						X	
10. Role of economic institutions												
11. Role of money	X	X										
12. Role of interest rates												
13. Role of resources in determining income			X						X	X		
14. Profit and the entrepreneur												
15. Growth												
16. Role of government												X
17. Using cost/benefit analysis to evaluate government programs												
18. Macroeconomy-income/employment, prices	X											
19. Unemployment and inflation				X								
20. Monetary and fiscal policy												

Happy Deal?

Mathematics Prerequisites

Prior to this lesson, students should know:
- A ratio compares two quantities.
- A proportion states that two ratios are equivalent.
- The Property of Proportions (Cross Products) can be applied to determine one missing value in a statement of proportion.
- How to state a part of a whole in terms of percent.
- How to find the mean (average).

Lesson Objectives

Students will be able to:
- Define *price, exchange rate, GDP,* and *per capita GDP.*
- Convert one currency into another, using exchange rates.
- Compare the percentage of income that the same product will require in different countries, using local currency.

Abstract

In this lesson, the students learn about currencies used in selected countries. They compare the prices of a Big Mac™ in different countries and convert the prices into U.S. dollars, using exchange rates. The students determine in which country a Big Mac™ is cheapest (a Happy Deal) and most expensive, in terms of U.S. dollars. Finally, the students calculate the percentage of daily income (per capita GDP per day) that is required in each country to purchase a Big Mac™ in terms of the local currency.

Mathematics Terms

- Fractions
- Percentages
- Rational numbers
- Bar graphs
- Proportional reasoning

Materials

- One copy of Activities 1.1–1.3 for each student
- Transparencies of Visuals 1.1–1.4
- Samples of foreign currency (optional)

Estimated Time

Two class periods

Day 1

Warm-Up Activities

1. Define ratio as the comparison of two quantities. A ratio can be written to compare any two quantities. Discuss the following examples.
   ▸ Fractions are ratios and compare the number of pieces being focused on to the number required to make the whole: 3/4 means focusing on three pieces out of four pieces that would make the whole.
   ▸ A ratio can describe how to mix fruit juice from concentrate: 3/1 means use three cans of water for every one can of concentrate.
   ▸ A ratio can describe how well a batter is doing in softball: 4/10 means a player got four hits and had ten at bats.

2. Define proportion as a statement of two equal ratios. Discuss the following examples.
   ▸ The fractions 3/4 and 6/8 represent the same part of a whole: 3/4 = 6/8.
   ▸ If you wanted to make three times the amount of the same type of juice, you would use the following amounts of water and concentrate: 3/1 = 9/3. Instead of three cans of water and one can of concentrate, you would use nine cans of water and three cans of concentrate.
   ▸ If a player got four hits for every ten at bats and she remains consistent and has a total of 100 at bats, you would expect her to get 40 hits: 4/10 = 40/100.

3. Remind the students how to find the missing part of a proportion, given the other three parts.
   ▸ Use the Property of Proportions (Cross Products) to find a missing value in a proportion.
   ▸ Write the following example, step-by-step, on the board. To find an equivalent fraction, if we know 3/7 = n/21, then:

$$3/7 = n/21$$
$$3(21) = 7n$$
$$63 = 7n$$
$$63/7 = 7n/7$$
$$9 = n$$

So, 3/7 = 9/21
   ▸ If we know that juice is made in the ratio of three cans of water to one can of concentrate, and we want to use four cans of concentrate, we can determine how much water to use.

$$3/1 \ = \ n/4$$
$$3(4) \ = \ n(1)$$
$$12 \ = \ n$$

So, $3/1 = 12/4$, and 12 cans of water should be used to make four times the amount of juice.

➤ If a softball player made four hits in 10 at bats, and if she kept playing consistently, how many hits she would have after 27 at bats can be predicted.

$$4/10 \ = \ n/27$$
$$4(27) \ = \ 10n$$
$$108 \ = \ 10n$$
$$108/10 \ = \ 10n/10$$
$$10.8 \ = \ n$$

So, $4/10 = 10.8/27$. This softball player could be expected to have about 11 hits after being at bat 27 times.

4. Use the Property of Proportions (Cross Products) to find the missing value in the following proportions.
   a. $3 / 8 = n / 24$ (n=9)
   b. $4 / 12 = 16 / n$ (n=48)
   c. $2 / 1.9 = 4 / n$ (n=3.8)
   d. $1.33 / n = 4 / 5$ (n=1.6625)

Procedures

1. Teach warm-up activity for Day 1.

2. Tell the students that there were McDonald's™ restaurants in 120 countries all over the world in 2001. Ask the students how they would pay for a Big Mac™ if they visited a McDonald's™ in Tokyo, Japan. (They would use yen, the Japanese currency.) Explain that most countries have their own currency (i.e., money).

3. Give a copy of Activity 1.1 to each student, and display Visual 1.1. Have the students identify the currency name for each country, using the visual and the clues on the activity. As the students identify the currency associated with each country, draw lines on the visual connecting the country to the name of its currency. (Australia-dollar, Canada-dollar, Chile-peso, China-yuan, Denmark-krone, France-franc, Germany-Deutsche mark, Indonesia-rupiah, Italy-lire, Japan-yen, Mexico-peso, Philippines-peso, Russia-ruble, South Africa-rand, Thailand-baht) Point out that several countries have the same name for their currencies. Display Visual 1.2, explaining that the United States, Australia, and Canada use the term "dollar," but the currencies actually are different despite the name in common.

4. Point out that students visiting England must convert their U.S. dollars to British pounds before buying a hamburger in London. Businesses in

England want to be paid in pounds, just as businesses in the United States want to be paid in dollars. Any student visiting England must buy pounds with dollars. Whenever people buy something, they pay a price for it. Define **price** as what people pay when they buy a good or service and what they receive when they sell a good or service.

5. Explain that when people convert the currency they hold for another currency, there is a price for the currency. An **exchange rate** is the price of one nation's currency in terms of another nation's currency. For example, in May 2001, one U.S. dollar was equal to 0.70 British pounds.

6. Write $1 = £.70 on the board and point out that it takes more than $1 to buy 1 British pound. Ask the following.
   a. How should the basic equation be written to represent the price equivalent of something priced in U.S. dollars? (Price in £/ £.70 = price in $/$1)
   b. If the price of a Big Mac™ were £3 in London, how many dollars would be required to buy one? [(£3/£.7) x $1 = $4.28)]
   c. If you knew that the price of a Big Mac™ was $2.54 in the United States, what price would you estimate for the hamburger in London? [($2.54/$1) x £.7 = £1.78]

7. Tell the students to work in pairs to complete more conversions for other products with different prices. For example, have them determine the "British pound" price of a $1,500 computer. (x/.7)=1,500/1=£1,050) When the students are finished, allow time for pairs to share their examples.

8. Distribute a copy of Activity 1.2 to each student. Tell the students to use the equation to fill in the empty boxes on the table. When the students are finished, display Visual 1.3 so that they can check their answers. Ask the following.
   a. In which country will you pay the most U.S. dollars to buy enough local currency to purchase a Big Mac™? (Denmark, where the dollar price is $2.93.)
   b. Where will you get a Happy Deal and pay less than the equivalent of $2.54? (In every country except Denmark, because the prices in U.S. dollars are lower than $2.54.)
   c. In which country do you get the Happiest Deal? (In the Philippines at $1.17.)

9. Ask the students if they think that Filipinos get a really Happy Deal. (Students are likely to respond that Filipinos do get a good deal at a price of $1.17.) Ask if they think that $2.54 is expensive for most Americans, so they're getting an unhappy deal. (Students are likely to respond that $2.54 is not a very high price.) Point out that whether a

price is considered expensive depends on how much income people have. A person with an income of $750 per month might find that eating out is too expensive after paying for rent, utilities, gasoline, taxes, and other basics.

10. Have the students speculate whether a Big Mac™ is likely to be considered expensive in other countries. (The students should use proportional reasoning to determine that the percentage of income spent on a hamburger in each country would provide a good basis for comparison among countries.) Summarize student ideas, pointing out that the students need an estimate of a person's income in each country to determine if the price of a Big Mac™ is a Happy Deal.

Day 2

Warm-Up Activities

1. Define percent as a way to express number relationships as "per hundred." Any ratio can be expressed as a percent. For example, 3/4 can be expressed as a percent because 3/4 = 75/100 = 0.75 = 75%.

2. Remind the students how to find the percent equivalent for any ratio. Ask the following.

   a. If a student is correct on 13 questions out of 20 on a quiz, how is the score determined as a percent? (13 out of 20 is expressed as the ratio 13/20. Divide the part of the test that was correct by the total number of test items. 13/20 = 0.65=65%)

   b. The student got 65% of the test questions correct. Use the same approach to determine the percent of the test items the student missed. (The student missed 7 out of 20 questions. 7/20 = 0.35 = 35%. This student got 35% of the test questions wrong.)

   c. Determine the percents in the following example. Stan went out with friends on Saturday and brought $22.00. He spent $7.26 on lunch and $9.70 to play miniature golf. Show the statements and resulting percents.

      ➤ What percent of his money did he spend on lunch? (7.26 out of 22.00 is expressed as 7.26/22. Divide the amount spent on lunch by the total amount of money. 7.26/22 = .33 = 33%. Stan spent 33% of his money on lunch.)

      ➤ What percent of his money did he spend on miniature golf? (9.70 out of 22.00 is expressed as 9.7/22. Divide the amount spent on miniature golf by the total amount of money. 9.7/22 = 44%. Stan spent 44% of his money on miniature golf.)

      ➤ What percent did he have left? (Subtract Stan's expenses from his amount of money. The remainder is the amount left over. 22.00 – 7.26 – 9.70 = 5.04. 5.04 out of 22.00 is expressed as

5.04/22.00. Divide the amount remaining after expenses by the total amount of money. 5.04 /22 = .23 = 23%. Stan did not spend 23% of the money he had.)

Procedures

1. Teach the Warm-up Activity for Day 2.

2. Give a copy of Activity 1.3 to each student. Explain that GDP stands for Gross Domestic Product. **GDP** is a basic measure of a nation's economic output and income. GDP represents income generated by the entire economy. Ask the students how to calculate the average income of a person in the country.

   (Divide the GDP by the population.)

   Explain that the average income per person is called **per capita GDP** (capita = person). Lead a discussion on whether the average income defines exactly what each person in the country receives in one year.

   (No. Some people will receive more, some less. Some people are young children who don't receive income, and some people may be unable or choose not to earn income. An average is a rough estimate—a summary statistic. It provides no details about each individual.)

3. Be sure to point out that each number in the second column is stated in terms of the local currency. For example, per capita GDP is 7585.69 yuan in China. In Indonesia, per capita GDP is 6,831,603.59 rupiahs. Have the students state the per capita GDP in each country in its currency.

   (For example, 37,160.83 dollars in the U.S.; 50,070.91 Deutsche marks in Germany, etc.)

4. Point out that the purchase price of one Big Mac™ probably represents a very small percentage of a person's income for an entire year. The percent of daily income required to buy a Big Mac would provide a better comparison. Ask the students how to determine the daily income, given the yearly income.

   (Daily income is determined by dividing GDP per capita by 365.)

   Tell the students to compute the daily income in the third column.

5. Remind the students that the fourth column shows the prices of a Big Mac™ in each country's currency. Have the students complete the fifth column to determine the percent of daily income that a Big Mac™ would comprise. Display Visual 1.4 so that they can check their answers.

6. Discuss the following.
   a. In which country does a Big Mac™ take the smallest percent of daily income? (United States at 2.5%)
   b. In which country does a Big Mac™ take the largest percent of daily income? (Indonesia at 78.5%)
   c. Describe the advantage of using the percents in the fifth column to determine if the purchase of a Big Mac™ is a Happy Deal for people who live in that country rather than using the price of a Big Mac™. (A price comparison is meaningless because all currencies are not equal; i.e., one dollar is not equal to one rupiah is not equal to one yuan and so forth. A percent that compares the price of the good relative to income provides an equal basis for comparison.)
   d. In which countries might a Big Mac™ be considered to be a luxury? Why? (In Indonesia, China, and the Philippines, because it takes a large percent of daily income which would require a person to forgo a lot of other goods.)
   e. Describe a way to determine if a product is relatively expensive in one country compared to another country. (Calculate the percent of income required to purchase the product.)

7. (Optional) Have the students create a bar graph representing the percentage of daily income required to purchase a Big Mac™ by country.

8. Summarize the main points of the lesson with the following points.
   ➤ Every country has its own currency. (NOTE: CHANGES HAVE OCCURRED IN THE EUROPEAN UNION WITH THE DEVELOPMENT OF A SINGLE EU CURRENCY, THE EURO.)
   ➤ A price is what people pay when they buy a good or service and what they receive when they sell a good or service.
   ➤ An exchange rate is the price of one nation's currency in terms of another nation's currency.
   ➤ Gross domestic product (GDP) is a basic measure of a nation's economic output and income.
   ➤ Per capita GDP is GDP divided by the number of people living in a country.
   ➤ Ratios are used to identify exchange rates, which are comparisons of relations.
   ➤ Proportions state that two ratios are equivalent.
   ➤ The Property of Proportions (Cross Products) can be used to find a missing value in a statement of proportion.

ACTIVITY 1.1 ▲ Countries and Currencies

Use the transparency and the following clues to match a country with its currency.

Clue	Country	Currency
1. I went DOWN UNDER and paid 25 dollars to see the Great Barrier Reef.		
2. I visited Thailand and PURCHASED some ma-muang (mango) to eat.		
3. I went to MANILA and spent my pesos on a silver filigree necklace.		
4. For our special dinner, my mother used her BEST DISHES that she bought for 3,000 yuan.		
5. The rupiah is the currency in the COUNTRY that is comprised of more than 13,000 tropical islands.		
6. In COPENHAGEN, you pay with a currency whose name comes from the Latin word for "CROWN."		
7. In the FIFTY STATES, students holler, "Oh, Mom, can I have a . . . .?"		
8. Way down SOUTH OF THE BORDER, people PAY SO they can eat what they order.		
9. In this COUNTRY, Oh, Mama Mia, buy a pizza with your		
10. Listen to the U.S. national anthem at baseball games in MONTREAL, but use this country's CURRENCY to buy peanuts and Cracker Jack.		
11. This COUNTRY goes from sea to sea, and ruble is its currency.		
12. Pesos will buy a stew of meat, beans, and tomatoes in this COUNTRY.		
13. Let me be CANDID, you should visit Voltaire's home in PARIS.		
14. I have a DESIRE to see the Buddhist shrines in KYOTO.		
15. CAPETOWN's beaches have beautiful sand, buy soft drinks for only four		
16. This COUNTRY's currency sounds like it's from Holland, but it misses the mark.		

ACTIVITY 1.2 ▲ Big Mac™ Prices on April 17, 2001

Congratulations! You recently received a large inheritance. Now you plan to travel around the world. In each country, you intend to visit McDonald's™ and eat a Big Mac™, your favorite fast food. You did some research on the Internet and were able to retrieve the data in the table below. Now you must make some calculations and complete the table.

Country	Currency	Price of Big Mac in Local Currency	Exchange Rate* 1 US$ =	Price in U.S. Dollars
United States	Dollar	2.54	1.00	2.54
Australia	Dollar	3.00	1.98	1.52
Canada	Dollar	3.33		2.14
Chile	Peso	1,260.00	601.00	
China	Yuan	9.90	8.28	
Denmark	Krone	24.75	8.46	
France	Franc	18.50	7.44	
Germany	Deutsche mark	5.10		2.30
Indonesia	Rupiah	14,700.00	10,855.00	
Italy	Lire	4,300.00	2,195.00	
Japan	Yen	294.00	124.00	
Mexico	Peso	21.90	9.29	
Philippines	Peso	59.00		1.17
Russia	Ruble	35.00		1.21
South Africa	Rand	9.70	8.13	
Thailand	Baht	55.00	45.50	

*Exchange rate on April 17, 2001

Source: "Big Mac Currencies," The Economist, April 19, 2001.

ACTIVITY 1.3 ▲ Happy Deal?

Country	GDP (Per Capita) 2001 in Local Currency	Daily Income (365 Days)	Price of Big Mac™ in Local Currency	% of Daily Income to Purchase One Big Mac™
United States	37,160.83		2.54	
Australia	35,080.01		3.00	
Canada	34,889.51		3.33	
Chile	2,764,091.46		1,260.00	
China	7585.69		9.90	
Denmark	256,160.88		24.75	
France	160,411.91		18.50	
Germany	50,070.91		5.10	
Indonesia	6,831,603.59		14,700.00	
Italy	41,728,127.90		4,300.00	
Japan	4,025,635.92		294.00	
Mexico	57,663.05		21.90	
Philippines	47,615.59		59.00	
Russia	57,743.63		35.00	
South Africa	21,355.90		9.70	
Thailand	81,073.58		55.00	

*Per capita GDP per day

Source: IMF World Economic Outlook Database (estimated GDP for 2001).

VISUAL 1:1 ▲ Make the Connection

Australia	
Canada	
Chile	Baht
China	Deutsche Mark
Denmark	Dollar
France	Franc
Germany	Krone
Indonesia	Lire
Italy	Peso
Japan	Rand
Mexico	Ruble
Philippines	Rupiah
Russia	Yen
South Africa	Yuan
Thailand	
United States	

South Africa —— Rand

VISUAL 1.2 ▲ Dollars in the World

Australia

Canada

United States

VISUAL 1.3 ▲ Answers to Activity 1.2

Country	Currency	Price of Big Mac in Local Currency	Exchange Rate * 1 US$ =	Price in U.S. Dollars
United States	Dollar	2.54	1.00	2.54
Australia	Dollar	3.00	1.98	1.52
Canada	Dollar	3.33	1.56	2.14
Chile	Peso	1,260	601.00	2.10
China	Yuan	9.90	8.28	1.20
Denmark	Krone	24.75	8.46	2.93
France	Franc	18.50	7.44	2.49
Germany	Deutsche mark	5.10	2.22	2.30
Indonesia	Rupiah	14,700.00	10,855.00	1.35
Italy	Lire	4,300.00	2,195.00	1.96
Japan	Yen	294.00	124.00	2.37
Mexico	Peso	21.90	9.29	2.36
Philippines	Peso	59.00	50.43	1.17
Russia	Ruble	35.00	28.90	1.21
South Africa	Rand	9.70	8.13	1.19
Thailand	Baht	55.00	45.50	1.21

*Exchange rate on April 17, 2001

Source: "Big Mac Currencies," The Economist, April 19, 2001.

VISUAL 1.4 ▲ Answers to Activity 1.3

Country	GDP (Per Capita) 2001 in Local Currency	Daily Income (365 Days)*	Price of Big Mac™ in Local Currency	% of Daily Income to Purchase One Big Mac™
United States	37,160.83	101.81	2.54	2.5
Australia	35,080.01	96.11	3.00	3.1
Canada	34,889.51	95.59	3.33	3.5
Chile	2,764,091.46	7572.85	1,260.00	16.6
China	7585.69	20.78	9.90	47.6
Denmark	256,160.88	701.81	24.75	3.5
France	160,411.91	439.49	18.50	4.2
Germany	50,070.91	137.18	5.10	3.7
Indonesia	6,831,603.59	18,716.72	14,700.00	78.5
Italy	41,728,127.90	114,323.63	4,300.00	3.8
Japan	4,025,635.92	11,029.14	294.00	2.7
Mexico	57,663.05	157.98	21.90	13.9
Philippines	47,615.59	130.45	59.00	45.2
Russia	57,743.63	158.20	35.00	22.1
South Africa	21,355.90	58.51	9.70	16.6
Thailand	81,073.58	222.12	55.00	24.8

*Per capita GDP per day

Source: IMF WEO Database (per capita GDP calculated using exchange rates).

Vacation Vexation

Mathematics Prerequisites

Prior to this lesson, students should know:
> A ratio compares two quantities.
> A proportion states that two ratios are equivalent.
> The Property of Proportions (Cross Products) can be applied to determine one missing value in a statement of proportion.
> How to state a part of a whole in terms of percent.

Lesson Objectives

Students will be able to:
> Define *exchange rate, foreign exchange, appreciation*, and *depreciation*.
> Convert one currency into another, using exchange rates.
> Determine if a currency has depreciated or appreciated when an exchange rate changes.
> Analyze the effects of currency depreciation/appreciation.

Abstract

In this lesson, the students listen to the story of an American girl who is planning a trip to Mexico. They learn about foreign exchange and compare exchange rates to determine if one currency has appreciated or depreciated against another currency. Using proportional reasoning, they determine the monetary effects of currency appreciation and depreciation. They analyze how changes in exchange rates affect the prices of goods and services from another country.

Mathematics Terms

> Percentages
> Rational numbers
> Proportional reasoning

Materials

> One copy of Activities 2.1 and 2.2 for each student
> Transparencies of Visuals 2.1–2.3

Estimated Time

Two class periods

Warm-Up Activities

NOTE: If you have taught lesson 1, this warm-up activity may not be necessary.

1. Define ratio as the comparison of two quantities. A ratio can be written to compare any two quantities. Discuss the following.
   - Fractions are ratios and compare the number of pieces being focused on to the number required to make the whole. 3/4 means four pieces would make the whole, but the focus is on only three parts.
   - A ratio can describe how to mix ingredients to make something. 2/1 means two cups of flour are required for every one cup of salt in a homemade play dough recipe.
   - A ratio can describe how well a student performs on a quiz. 19/20 means that the student got 19 out of 20 quiz questions correct.

2. Define proportion as a statement of two equal ratios. Discuss the following examples.
   - The fractions 3/4 and 6/8 represent the same part of a whole: 3/4= 6/8.
   - If you wanted to make four times the amount of homemade play dough, you would use the following amounts of flour and salt in the recipe: 2/1 = 8/4. Instead of two cups of flour and one cup of salt, you would use eight cups of flour and four cups of salt.
   - If a student got 19 out of 20 quiz questions right, and if she remained consistent in her performance on the next quiz, which has 40 questions, we might expect her to perform in the following way: 19/20 = 38/40. She could expect to get 38 out of 40 points on the next quiz.

3. Remind the students how to find the missing part of a proportion, given the other three parts.
   - Use the Property of Proportions (Cross Products) to find a missing value in a proportion with the following examples.
   - Write the following example, step-by-step, on the board. To find an equivalent fraction, if we know 3/8 = n/24:

$$
\begin{aligned}
3/8 &= n/24 \\
3(24) &= 8n \\
72 &= 8n \\
72/8 &= 8n/8 \\
9 &= n
\end{aligned}
$$

   - If we know that some of the play dough ingredients are to be mixed in the ratio of 2 cups of flour to 1 cup of salt and we want to triple the recipe, we can determine how much of each ingredient to use.

$$
\begin{aligned}
2/1 &= n/3 \\
2(3) &= n(1) \\
6 &= n
\end{aligned}
$$

> ▸ If a student has 15 questions right out of 18, and if he keeps performing consistently, we can predict how well he will do on a quiz with 45 questions on it.
>
> $$15/18 \ = \ n/45$$
> $$15(45) \ = \ 18n$$
> $$675 \ = \ 18n$$
> $$675/18 \ = \ 18n/18$$
> $$37.5 \ = \ n$$
>
> So, $15/18 = 37.5/45$. We would expect this student to get 37 or 38 questions right out of a total of 45 questions.

Procedures

1. Read the following scenario to the class.

   María Ramirez thinks that she's the luckiest girl alive! Her aunt who lives in Mexico has invited her and her older sister to visit. Her grandmother just announced that she's giving María $1,440 as a high school graduation present ($120 for each year in school) for a trip to Mexico to visit her aunt and cousins. María will stay for one week, and she must determine if she has enough money. She went to the Internet to get information and determined her expenses.

2. Display a copy of Visual 2.1 and continue reading María's story.

   María ran to her parents crying, "I can't go to Mexico! The cost of a trip to Mexico is $7,829.20, and that's without airfare, souvenirs, or any unexpected expenses. Only rich people can afford to go to Mexico!" María's father turned to her mother and asked, "How do you solve a problem like María's?" "No problem," her mother said calmly, "that's the total in pesos, not dollars." María laughed and said, "Oh, yeah! I forgot that the peso is the money in Mexico. Nevermind! Oh, by the way, what's the exchange rate?"

3. Point out that most countries have their own currencies. In the United States, the currency is the U.S. dollar; it's the peso in Mexico, the yuan in China, the Canadian dollar in Canada, the rand in South Africa, and the bolivar in Venezuela. The prices of goods and services in each country are stated in the country's currency.

4. Define **exchange rate** as the price of one nation's currency in terms of another nation's currency, in this case, $1 = 9.2 pesos. Give a copy of Activity 2.1 to each student. Demonstrate how to calculate the dollar cost of the taxi using the following ratios on the board.

$$\frac{\$x}{\$1} = \frac{294.40 \text{ pesos}}{9.2 \text{ pesos}}$$

Assign Activity 2.1. When the students are finished, display Visual 2.2 to review the answers. Remind the students that María has only

$1,440 for the trip. Because her expenses are $1,701, she must make some changes. Ask the students for recommendations on how to make her vacation possible.

(Answers will vary, but the students are likely to suggest finding a cheaper hotel, less expensive meals, fewer souvenirs, bus transportation instead of taxis, and so forth.)

5. Continue María's story, reading the following.

A week later María looked very unhappy at dinner. Her mother asked, "Qué tal, María?" María sighed, "Mom, guess what? I was doing some more research for my trip, and I discovered that the exchange rate has changed to $1 = 9.5 pesos! Now, what am I going to do? Everything gets more and more expensive!" María's mother said, "María, that's good news. Everything will be cheaper now because the dollar is stronger. That will lower your expenses, not increase them. Now you will divide the peso price by 9.5, a larger denominator. You can buy more pesos with each dollar, so goods and services in Mexico will be cheaper to you."

7. Now that the exchange rate is $1 = 9.5 pesos, María hopes that she has enough money to make the trip without cutting expenses. Discuss the following.
   a. Does she have enough money to cover all expenses for her trip? Explain how you know.

   (No. 7829.20 pesos divided by 9.5 pesos equals $824.13. Adding the other expenses not stated in pesos - $850, sums to a total of $1674.13. María only has $1,440.)

   b. What exchange rate will allow María to cover her anticipated expenses?

   (Given Maria's other expenses of $850, she must cover all the rest with $590 ($1,440-$850). She needs an exchange rate that will convert 7829.20 pesos into $590. 7829.20/590 = 13.3. The exchange rate would have to be $1 = 13.3 pesos.)

8. Point out that people in a country want to be paid in their nation's currency. If U.S. students go to a movie theater, they must pay for the ticket and snacks in U.S. dollars. If U.S. students go to a movie theater in Mexico, they must pay for the ticket and snacks in Mexican pesos. Ask the students how they might get pesos.

(The students may respond that they would go to a bank. Some students may have visited another country and know that they can get the foreign currency at a bank, at an airport exchange office, or at an exchange office in a city.)

9. Explain that almost every international exchange of goods and services requires the exchange of one currency for another. Most international transactions involve foreign exchange. **Foreign exchange** is all
currencies other than a nation's currency. U.S. dollars are foreign
exchange to Mexicans; pesos are foreign exchange for Americans.
Ask the students for other examples of foreign exchange for Americans.

(Pesos, rubles, yuan, Euros, yen, and currencies of other countries.)

10. Tell the students that currencies are bought and sold in a foreign
exchange market (known as "forex") to help facilitate trade and other
international transactions. Prices of goods and services are determined in markets by the interaction of the buyers and sellers. The
same is true in a foreign exchange market. Ask the following.
   a. If black jeans became very popular among American teenagers,
   what do you predict will happen to the price of black jeans? (The
   price will increase because of greater demand for black jeans.)
   b. Suppose that American black jeans became very popular among
   European teenagers. What would happen to the demand for
   American black jeans? (It would increase.)
   c. If European teenagers want to buy these jeans, what will European clothing stores do? (They'll buy American black jeans to put
   in their stores.)
   d. What will the European clothing businesses need in order to buy
   American black jeans? (They'll need to buy U.S. dollars to buy
   black jeans from American manufacturers.)
   e. If American products are in greater demand in Europe, what will
   happen to the demand for U.S. dollars? (It will increase because
   Europeans will need more U.S. dollars to buy the products.)
   f. Will it take more or fewer Euros to buy a dollar? (More.) So, what
   happens to the price of a U.S. dollar in terms of the Euro? (It will
   increase; that is, it will take more Euros to buy one U.S. dollar.)
   Explain that the price of the dollar increased, just as the price of
   black jeans increased, because of greater demand.

11. Remind the students that María discovered that the exchange rate
changed from $1 = 9.2 pesos to $1 = 9.5 pesos. María thought that
this was a problem, but she was wrong. Have the students compute
the price of one peso for each exchange rate. [At $1 = 9.2 pesos, the
price of one peso is 10.9 cents (1/9.2 = .109). At $1 = 9.5 pesos, the
price of one peso is 10.5 cents (1/9.5 = .105)]

12. Explain that the dollar is stronger (relative to the peso) because it can
buy more pesos. When comparing the dollar against the peso, the
dollar has appreciated in value, and the peso has depreciated in value.
Appreciation of a currency means that people can exchange that

currency for more of another currency. In this example, one dollar will purchase more pesos, 9.5 instead of 9.2. **Depreciation** of a currency means that people can exchange that currency for less of another currency. In María's case, the peso is weaker (relative to the dollar) because it can buy fewer dollars. One peso buys $.105 or 10.5 cents instead of $.109 or 10.9 cents.

13. Point out that currencies appreciate and depreciate continually on the foreign exchange market. Give a copy of Activity 2.2 to each student and assign it to the student to complete. Display Visual 2.3 and discuss answers when the students have finished.

14. Summarize the main points of the lesson with the following.
    ➤ Almost every nation has its own currency. In the U. S., it is the dollar. In Mexico, it's the peso. In the European Union, member countries share a single currency, the Euro.
    ➤ An exchange rate is the price of one nation's currency in terms of another nation's currency.
    ➤ When an exchange rate between two countries changes, one currency will become more valuable, and the other currency will become less valuable relative to one another.
    ➤ When one currency becomes more valuable against another currency, the currency appreciates. When the other currency becomes less valuable, the currency depreciates.
    ➤ When a currency appreciates against another currency, it takes fewer currency units to buy a given unit of the other currency. For example, if the dollar appreciates relative to the yen, it takes fewer dollars to buy a given amount of yen. The converse is true when a currency depreciates.
    ➤ When a currency appreciates, goods and services in the other country become cheaper. For example, if the dollar appreciates relative to the Japanese yen, Japanese goods will be cheaper to Americans who have dollars.
    ➤ When a currency depreciates, goods and services in the other country become more expensive. For example, if the Japanese yen depreciates against the dollar, American goods are more expensive to people who have yen.
    ➤ Ratios compare two amounts.
    ➤ Proportions state that two ratios are equivalent.
    ➤ The Property of Proportions (Cross Products) can be used to find a missing value in a statement of proportion.

ACTIVITY 2.1 ▲ How Much Does It REALLY Cost?

María went to the Internet and estimated the following costs of her trip to Mexico. After realizing that the prices were stated in Mexican pesos, María conducted research and found that the exchange rate was $1 = 9.2 pesos. Using this exchange rate, calculate the total amount of dollars required for María's expenses.

Day	Item	Price in Pesos	Price in Dollars
JUNE 6-8 MEXICO CITY			
June 6	Airfare to Mexico City (roundtrip)		400.00
June 6	Taxi to hotel	294.40	
June 6	Hotel room	598.00	
June 6	Dinner	138.00	
June 7	Breakfast, lunch, and dinner	276.00	
June 7	Hotel room	598.00	
June 7	Bus tour to Aztec pyramids	506.00	
June 7	Taxi and tickets to the ballet	276.00	
JUNE 8-10 GUADALAJARA			
June 8	Breakfast	46.00	
June 8	Airfare to Guadalajara (roundtrip) to visit cousin Antonio and his family		250.00
June 8	Take cousin and family out to dinner (7)	966.00	
JUNE 10-13 MEXICO CITY			
June 10	Return to Mexico City–hotel room	598.00	
June 10	Taxi to hotel	294.40	
June 10	Dinner	138.00	
June 11	Breakfast, lunch, dinner	276.00	
June 11	Taxis and tickets to Chapultepec Park for the museums and to Constitution Plaza to see the cathedral	276.00	
June 11	Guided tour to Garibaldi Plaza to hear the mariachi bands	368.00	
June 11	Hotel room	598.00	
June 12	Breakfast, lunch, and dinner	276.00	
June 12	Guided Tour to Xochimilco gardens and the Basilica of Guadalupe	368.00	
June 12	Hotel room	598.00	
June 13	Breakfast	46.00	
June 13	Taxi to airport	294.40	
OTHER			
	Souvenirs		100.00
	Miscellaneous		100.00
	TOTAL		

ACTIVITY 2.2 ▲ Currency Currents

Read each headline from *Currency Currents* newspaper, and answer the questions.

More Europeans choose U.S. vacations as Euro rises

Popular American resorts, such as Walt Disney World®, are increasingly popular with Europeans looking for vacation bargains.

---

1. This headline says that the U.S. dollar has **depreciated appreciated** (circle one) against the Euro, and the Euro has **depreciated appreciated** (circle one) against the dollar.

2. Given your response to Question #1, if people in Paris want to buy U.S. computers, will they be more expensive or less expensive? Explain your answer.

3. If the exchange rate was 0.86 € = $1.00 a year earlier, according to the headline, which of the following could have happened? Explain your answers.

   _____ 0.84 € = $1.00   _____ 0.86 € = $0.98
   _____ 0.90 € = $1.00   _____ 0.86 € = $1.03

Yen down 2% as Japan's economy weakens

Ongoing concerns about the Japanese economy weakened the yen further against the dollar. The yen slipped to 122.5 yen from 120 a month ago.

---

4. Will Americans who plan to visit Japan have a less expensive or more expensive trip? Explain your answer.

5. Will Japanese consumers of products "made in the USA" have to pay more or less for the American products? Explain your answer.

VISUAL 2.1 ▲ Maria's Mix Up

Day	Item	Expense
	JUNE 6-8 MEXICO CITY	
June 6	Airfare to Mexico City (roundtrip)	
June 6	Taxi to hotel	294.40
June 6	Hotel room	598.00
June 6	Dinner	138.00
June 7	Breakfast, lunch, and dinner	276.00
June 7	Hotel room	598.00
June 7	Bus tour to Aztec pyramids	506.00
June 7	Taxi and tickets to the folklore ballet	276.00
	JUNE 8-10 GUADALAJARA	
June 8	Breakfast	46.00
June 8	Airfare to Guadalajara (roundtrip) to visit cousin Antonio and his family	
June 8	Take cousin and family out to dinner (7)	966.00
	JUNE 10-13 MEXICO CITY	
June 10	Return to Mexico City–hotel room	598.00
June 10	Transportation to hotel	294.40
June 10	Dinner	138.00
June 11	Breakfast, lunch, dinner	276.00
June 11	Taxis and tickets to Chapultepec Park for the museums and to Constitution Plaza to see the cathedral	276.00
June 11	Guided tour to Garibaldi Plaza to hear the mariachi bands	368.00
June 11	Hotel room	598.00
June 12	Breakfast, lunch, and dinner	276.00
June 12	Guided Tour to Xochimilco gardens and the Basilica of Guadalupe	368.00
June 12	Hotel room	598.00
June 13	Breakfast	46.00
June 13	Taxi to airport	294.40
OTHER		
	Souvenirs	
	Miscellaneous	
	TOTAL	7829.20

VISUAL 2.2 ▲ Answers to Activity 2.1

Day	Item	Price in Pesos	Price in Dollars
JUNE 6-8 MEXICO CITY			
June 6	Airfare to Mexico City (roundtrip)		400.00
June 6	Taxi to hotel	294.40	32.00
June 6	Hotel room	598.00	65.00
June 6	Dinner	138.00	15.00
June 7	Breakfast, lunch, and dinner	276.00	30.00
June 7	Hotel room	598.00	65.00
June 7	Bus tour to Aztec pyramids	506.00	55.00
June 7	Taxi and tickets to the ballet	276.00	30.00
JUNE 8-10 GUADALAJARA			
June 8	Breakfast	46.00	5.00
June 8	Airfare to Guadalajara (roundtrip) to visit cousin Antonio and his family		250.00
June 8	Take cousin and family out to dinner (7)	966.00	105.00
JUNE 10-13 MEXICO CITY			
June 10	Return to Mexico City–hotel room	598.00	65.00
June 10	Transportation to hotel	294.40	32.00
June 10	Dinner	138.00	15.00
June 11	Breakfast, lunch, dinner	276.00	30.00
June 11	Taxis and tickets to Chapultepec Park for the museums and to Constitution Plaza to see the cathedral	276.00	30.00
June 11	Guided tour to Garibaldi Plaza to hear the mariachi bands	368.00	40.00
June 11	Hotel room	598.00	65.00
June 12	Breakfast, lunch, and dinner	276.00	30.00
June 12	Guided Tour to Xochimilco gardens and the Basilica of Guadalupe	368.00	40.00
June 12	Hotel room	598.00	65.00
June 13	Breakfast	46.00	5.00
June 13	Taxi to airport	294.40	32.00
OTHER			
	Souvenirs		100.00
	Miscellaneous		100.00
	TOTAL		1701.00

VISUAL 2.3 ▲ Answers to Activity 2.2

1. The dollar has depreciated, and the Euro has appreciated.

2. Less expensive. The Euro has appreciated, thus buying more dollars per Euro than before.

3. 0.84 € = $1.00 because the depreciated dollar will not buy as many Euros. 0.86 € = $1.03 because the appreciated Euro can buy more dollars.

4. Americans will have a less expensive trip because of the appreciation of the dollar. A dollar will buy more yen, 122.5 instead of 120.

5. Japanese must pay more for American products because the depreciation of the yen means that it takes more yen to buy a dollar.

Baby-sitting Wages and Movie Prices

Mathematics Prerequisites

Prior to this lesson, students should be able to:

➤ Draw and use scatter plots.
➤ Draw a line of best fit.

Lesson Objectives

Students will be able to:

➤ Define *wage, income, price*, and *purchasing power*.
➤ Organize and analyze data on wages and prices.
➤ Explain correlation and cause and effect.
➤ Apply graphing skills to create scatter plots and lines of best fit.

Abstract

Through an analysis of data for baby-sitting wages (a price for labor) and the price of movie tickets since 1945, this lesson introduces the students to the idea that prices for goods, services, and resources change over time. The lesson provides the foundation for lessons on inflation and its impact on purchasing power over time. (See Lesson 4.) Students plot and analyze data to determine correlation, and recognize the difference between correlation and cause and effect. The economics involved in the lesson will require the students to define wage, price, and income.

Mathematics Terms

➤ Graphical representations of a data set
➤ Scatter plots
➤ Line of best fit
➤ Negative and positive
➤ Prediction
➤ Cause and effect

Materials

➤ One copy of Activities 3.1 and 3.3 for each student
   Note: *Activity 3.2 may be read to students in class or students may be asked to read it in class or for homework.*
➤ Transparencies of Visuals 3.1 and 3.2

Estimated Time

One class period

Warm-Up Activities

NOTE: The "Warm-Up Activity" can be given to students as a home-work assignment the day before the lesson is taught.

1. Distribute a copy of Activity 3.1 to each student. Tell the students to answer the questions.

2. Define correlation as an association between two variables. Explain that a correlation can be positive or negative. Two sets of data are positively correlated if, as the numbers in one set tend to increase, the numbers in the other set also tend to increase. For example, as people grow taller, their weights tend to increase. Two sets of data are negatively correlated if, as the numbers in one set tend to increase, the numbers in the other set tend to decrease. For example, as temperatures fall, people tend to eat fewer sno-cones.

3. Display a transparency of Visual 3.1 and discuss the following.
   a. What type of correlation, if any, exists for these data? (Negative.)
   b. How do you know? (As people get older (age increases), the number of movies they see decreases.)
   c. About how many movies does an average 25-year-old attend in a year? (10)
   d. From the data in the scatter plot, how old do you think a person is who attends 16 movies in a year? (22–23)
   e. From the data in the scatter plot, how many movies would you predict a 14-year-old would attend in a year? (Approximately 33.) A 30-year-old? (Approximately 1.)

Procedures

1. Discuss the following.
   a. How many of you baby-sit or plan to baby-sit in the future? (Answers will vary.)
   b. Why do you baby-sit? (Parents make me, to earn money, likes young children, etc.)
   c. Have any of you ever taken a baby-sitting course? (Answers will vary.) Why? (To learn what to do in emergencies, to learn how to take care of young children.)

2. Explain that today they will learn about a thirteen-year-old boy, John, who took a baby-sitting course and has been offered his first opportunity to baby-sit.

3. Read Activity 3.2 to the class. When finished, discuss the following.
   a. What is John's problem? (How much to charge for baby-sitting.)
   b. How much did John's grandmother charge for baby-sitting? (25 cents an hour.)

c. Why did John's cousin think that 25 cents was too little? (25 cents won't buy that much today.)

d. What did John's grandmother say about what 25 cents would buy? (25 cents was a lot of money back then; she could buy a lot with 25 cents.)

4. Explain that a **price** is the amount consumers pay for a good or service. Ask the students for prices that they have paid for various items such as a shirt, shoes, a backpack, and a candy bar. (Answers will vary.)

5. Point out that when people work they usually expect to be paid. The payment they receive for work (labor) is a **wage**. People work to earn income. **Income** is payments people earn when they sell productive resources in the economy. One type of productive resource that people sell is their labor or human resource. Wages are one type of income.

6. Give a copy of Activity 3.3 to each student. Have the students look at the table of data that John collected. Discuss the following.
   a. Describe what happens to the data over time. (Over time, the price of movie tickets and the hourly wage for baby-sitting increase.)
   b. If a person baby-sat 10 hours a month in 1955, how much income would he or she earn? ($.40 x 10 = $4.00) If a person baby-sat 10 hours in 1975, how much income would he or she earn? ($1.50 x 10 = $15.00)

7. Have the students answer the questions on Activity 3.3.

8. Display a transparency of Visual 3.2 and discuss the following.
   a. What type of correlation, if any, exists for these data? (Positive correlation.)
   b. How do you know that this type of correlation exists? (Both variables move in the same direction; the line of best fit is upward sloping from the axis to the right.)
   c. If movie ticket prices rise, will hourly baby-sitting wages rise? (Not necessarily.) Why? (The fact that the variables are correlated does not mean that a change in one causes a change in the other.)
   d. If hourly baby-sitting wages decline, will movie ticket prices decline? (Not necessarily.) Why? (The fact that the variables are correlated does not mean that a change in one causes a change in the other.)
   e. Based on the data, what do you think will happen to the price of movie ticket prices by 2010? (Increase.)
   f. Based on the data, what do you think will happen to baby-sitting wages by 2015? (Increase.)

9. Ask the students why they and other people want to earn income by baby-sitting or doing other work. (To buy goods and services.) Explain

that **purchasing power** is the ability to buy goods and services with a fixed amount of money. The greater the purchasing power, the more goods and services people can buy with their money. Prices affect purchasing power. For example, if the price of candy bars rises, can you buy more or fewer candy bars with the same amount of money? (Fewer.) Discuss the following.

a. During which time period does John's grandmother think she had more purchasing power, 1945 or today? (1945.)

b. Why does she think this? (She thinks that she was able to buy more goods and services with the money she earned in 1945 than she can buy today.)

c. Do you agree with her? Why? (Answers will vary.)

d. What kind of information do you think we need to be able to answer the question for certain? (Students must compare prices with the amount of income that she had to spend in those two time periods.)

Closure

Discuss the main points of the lesson.

1. What is a price? (The amount consumers pay to purchase a good or service.)

2. What is a wage? (A payment received for work.)

3. What is income? (Payments people earn for the resources, such as human resources (labor) they sell in the economy.)

4. Is there a relation between prices and wages? (Yes.)

5. What does it look like? (Positive, both go up over time.)

6. Do wages cause prices to rise? (Not necessarily.)

7. Do prices cause wages to rise? (Not necessarily.)

8. What is purchasing power? (The ability to buy goods and services with money; the more goods and services people can buy with their money, the greater their purchasing power. Prices affect purchasing power.)

ACTIVITY 3.1 ▲ Warm-Up

1. Use the data below to make a scatter plot on the graph paper provided on the next page. On the horizontal axis, plot the age of people surveyed, and on the vertical axis plot number of movies attended in one year. (On the horizontal axis start your graph at age 16.)

Age of People Surveyed	No. of Movies in a Year
16	31
17	28
17	24
18	26
18	24
19	20
20	16
21	12
22	12
22	20
23	15
24	12
24	16
25	8
25	12
26	10

2. What type of correlation, if any, exists for these data? How do you know?

3. About how many movies does an average 25-year-old attend in a year?

4. From the data in the scatter plot, how old do you think a person is who attends 16 movies in a year?

5. From the data in the scatter plot, how many movies would you predict a 14-year-old would attend in a year? A 30-year-old?

ACTIVITY 3.2 ▲ How Much Should I Charge?

"Mom, guess what?" John called as he came in the door after walking the dog on Saturday morning. "Mr. Williams in apartment 3 asked me to baby-sit in two weeks. This will be my first baby-sitting job since I took the baby-sitting course at the community center. Mr. Williams asked me how much I charge. I wasn't sure. I told him that I'd talk to you. What do you think?"

"I don't know, John. The last time I hired a baby-sitter for you, I paid $3.75 an hour. Let's see when was that? Oh, yes, that was just last week and you are pretty difficult for most baby-sitters," Mom said.

"Mom! You know that's not true. I haven't had a baby-sitter in at least two years, and I am never difficult!" John replied excitedly.

"Okay John, you know I was teasing you, don't you? It was at least two years ago that I paid a sitter. And I only had one child. Doesn't Mr. Williams have three young children?" Mom said.

"He has two children. One is a four-year-old and the other is a five-year-old. I hadn't thought about charging more for more children. Maybe I should," John said.

Mom answered, "I'm not sure how much to charge. Maybe you can ask some of your cousins when we are at Aunt Kathy's for grandmother's birthday party this afternoon. You did remember about the party, didn't you?" Mom asked.

"Yeah, Mom, I remember. I even made her card on the computer after school yesterday like you asked. That's a pretty good idea, asking my cousins. I am pretty sure that Will, Tina, Tyrone, and Brittany still baby-sit. They can give me a good idea," John said.

At the party, while people were gathered around tables eating lunch, John brought up his baby-sitting problem. John was right. His cousins were helpful. They told him the prices they charged for baby-sitting. John borrowed some paper and a pen from Aunt Kathy so he could write the information down for later. After he and his cousins talked for a while, the whole family got into the discussion. His great Uncle Sam, grandmother's brother said, "Why, when I was young, people didn't pay baby-sitters. I took care of the children next door because we were neighbors and friends." Grandma said, "Sam that's not true. Sometimes I was paid for baby-sitting. Why, I earned $ .25 an hour. I worked 5 hours a week. That was a lot of money. I saved some and still had plenty to spend on fun things like a movie and popcorn."

"Grandma," John said, "You have got to be joking! Twenty-five cents is nothing! You can't even buy a candy bar for that. I am surprised that you would baby sit for that amount. Baby-sitting is a lot of work. The people that you baby-sat for didn't pay you enough."

"John, you'd be surprised what I could buy with twenty-five cents then. I could buy a movie ticket or some ground beef. Back then money was worth something. Not like today when prices are so high," Grandma answered.

"I believe you Grandma. I guess I'm just surprised. I think I'll talk with some of the other relatives and see what they think," John said.

He spoke with great-aunts and uncles, aunts and uncles, older cousins, and other relatives. As he listened, John jotted down information about baby-sitting wages and movie prices in the notebook that Aunt Kathy gave him.

On the way home, John said to his mom, "I guess Grandma was right. Almost everyone said they could buy more with their money when they were younger. I really don't understand that. They certainly didn't earn as much for baby-sitting as I will."

ACTIVITY 3.3 ▲ It's All Relative

The table below contains the data that John collected from his relatives.

Year	Baby-sitting Price (Wage) Per Hour	Movie Ticket Prices
1945	$.25	$.25
1950	.35	.60
1955	.40	.75
1960	.50	1.00
1965	.60	1.25
1970	.90	1.75
1975	1.50	2.50
1980	2.00	3.00
1985	2.50	3.25
1990	2.75	5.00
1995	3.00	5.50
2000	4.00	6.00

1. Use the space below to draw a scatter plot of the relationship between baby-sitting wages and movie ticket prices.

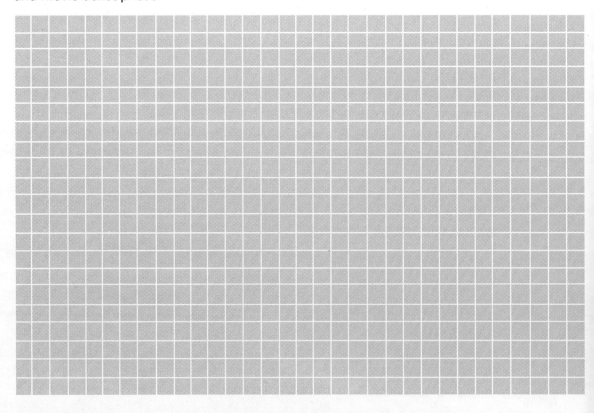

ACTIVITY 3.3 (continued)

2. Draw a line of best fit and answer the questions that follow.

3. What type of correlation, if any, exists for these data?

4. How do you know that this type of correlation exists?

5. If movie ticket prices rise, do you think hourly baby-sitting wages will also rise? Why?

6. If hourly baby-sitting wages decline, do you think movie ticket prices will also decline? Why?

7. Based on the data, what will happen to the price of movie tickets in 2010?

8. Based on the data, what will happen to baby-sitting wages in 2015?

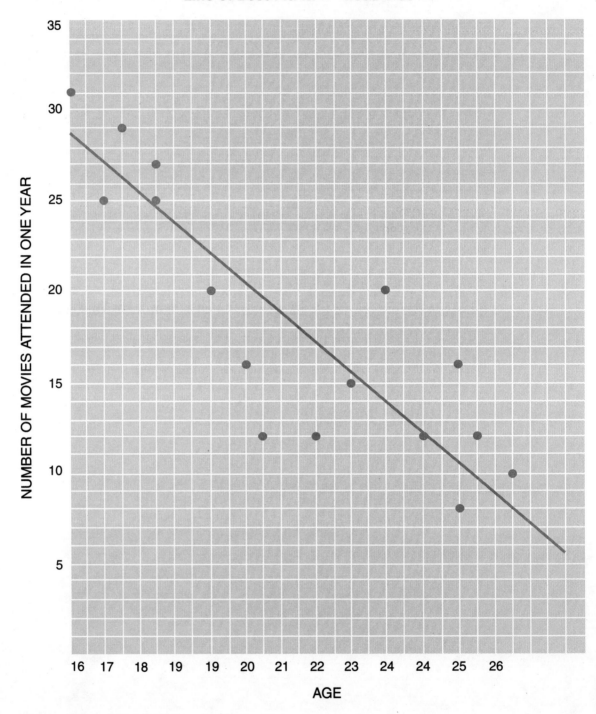

Line of Best Fit: m = −1.93a + 58

NUMBER OF MOVIES ATTENDED IN ONE YEAR

AGE

2. What type of correlation, if any, exists for these data? How do you know?

   Negative. In general, as age increases, the number of movies attended decreases.

3. About how many movies does an average 25-year-old attend in a year?

   About 10.

4. From the data in the scatter plot, how old do you think a person is who attends 16 movies in a year?

   From the data, we could expect such a person to be between 22 to 23 years old.

5. From the data in the scatter plot, how many movies would you predict a 14-year-old would attend in a year? If the trend continues, which is unlikely, a 14-year old might attend about 33 movies. A 30-year-old? If the trend continues, a 30-year old might attend, at most, one movie.

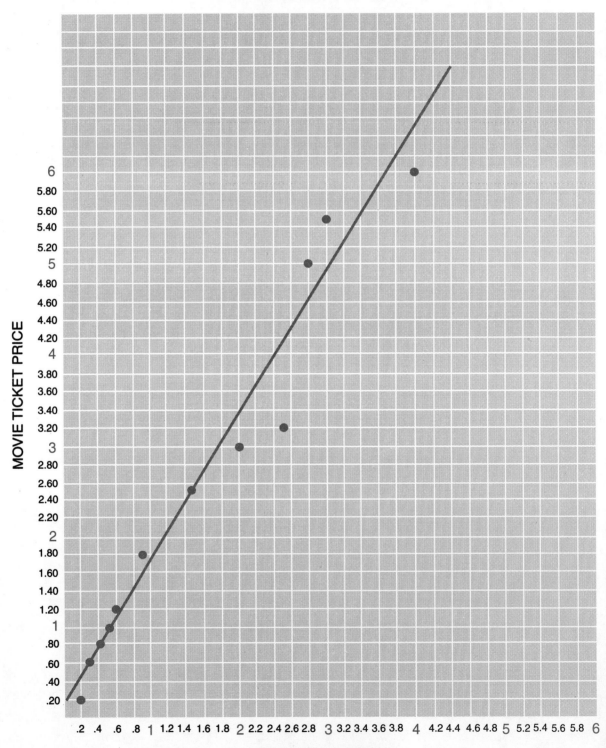

Line of Best Fit: p = 1.6w + .14
One-half Centimeter Grid

MOVIE TICKET PRICE

BABY-SITTING WAGE

VISUAL 3.2 (continued)

2. Draw a line of best fit and answer the questions that follow.

3. What type of correlation, if any, exists for these data?

    Positive correlation.

4. How do you know that this type of correlation exists?

    As the wages paid to baby-sitters increases, so does the price of movie tickets.

5. If movie ticket prices rise, do you think hourly baby-sitting wages will also rise? Why?

    Not necessarily. The fact that the variables are correlated does not mean that a change in one causes a change in the other.

6. If hourly baby-sitting wages decline, do you think movie ticket prices will also decline? Why?

    Not necessarily. The fact that the variables are correlated does not mean that a change in one causes a change in the other.

7. Based on the data, what will happen to the price of movie tickets in 2010?

    Increase.

8. Based on the data, what will happen to baby-sitting wages in 2015?

    Increase.

Constructing and Using a Consumer Price Index

Mathematics Prerequisites

Prior to this lesson, students be able to:
> Work flexibly with percents.
> Find percent increase or decrease given actual data.
> Find actual increase or decrease given the percent increase or decrease.

Lesson Objectives

Students will be able to:
> Define *inflation, purchasing power, real price, real wages, nominal price*, and *nominal wages*.
> Calculate percent change.
> Construct a price index.
> Describe the consumer price index (CPI).
> Explain how inflation affects purchasing power.

Abstract

In this lesson, the students look at data for baby-sitting wages (a price for labor) and the price of movie tickets over time. They learn about the Consumer Price Index and how to construct a price index. They learn how a price index is used to compare incomes and prices of goods and services from year to year. They define nominal and real prices and wages.

Mathematics Terms

> Percent change
> Basic computation

Materials

> One copy of Activity 4.1 for each group of 2-3 students
> One copy of Visual 4.3 for each student (optional)
> Transparencies of Visuals 4.1–4.5
> 1 computer with Internet access for each group of 2-3 students (Information is provided to complete the exercise if Internet access is not available.)
> One piece of graph paper for each student
> 2 different-colored pencils for each student

Estimated Time

Two class periods

Warm-Up Activities

1. Read the following scenario.

   Jill earns income in the summer by doing odd jobs in the neighbor-hood. She quickly learns that she can make more money–as long as she's willing to do the work! In her first week, Jill earned $75. After her second week, she noticed that her weekly earnings had increased to $101.25.

2. Discuss the following.
   a. What percent increase is this over the first week? (35%)
   b. In the third week, Jill had swimming lessons, so her earnings dropped to $25.30. By what percent did her earnings decrease? (75%)
   c. In the fourth week, Jill was motivated to earn more income again. At the end of the week she saw that her earnings had increased by 75% again. Does this mean that she earns as much as in her second week? (No, because she now earns $44.28, an increase of $18.98.)
   d. Jill had a two-week vacation with her family. She really enjoyed spending some of her income on lots of souvenirs and entertainment. In her first week after vacation, she earned $50. In her second week after vacation, she earned only $30. What percent of decrease does this represent? (40%)

Procedures

1. Explain that the **purchasing power** of a person's income is the amount of goods and services the person can buy with that amount of income. Prices affect people's purchasing power. Display the hypothetical data in Visual 4.1, and have the students speculate (not calculate) in which year people had more purchasing power.

2. Tell the students to use the data from Visual 4.1 to calculate how much someone who baby-sits for ten hours would earn in 1950 ($3.50), 1960 ($5.00), 1970 ($9.00), and 1980 ($20.00).

   Have the students compute how many movie tickets a person with that amount of income could purchase in 1950 (3.50/.60 = 5.83 or 5 tickets), 1960 (5.00/1.00 = 5 tickets), 1970 (9.00/1.75 = 5.14 or 5 tickets), and 1980 (20.00/3.00 = 6.67 or 6 tickets).

   Discuss the following.
   a. Based on your calculations, in which of these four years was the purchasing power the greatest? (1980)
   b. Is this what you expected? (Probably not.) Why? (We usually hear people say that they were better off in the old days.)

   c. What can we conclude about the relationship between wages and movie ticket prices between 1950 and 1980? (Generally wages rose as fast as, or a little faster than, movie ticket prices between 1950 and 1980.)

3. Explain that most people are concerned about the purchasing power of their income; that is, how many desired goods and services they can buy. If prices rise five percent and a person's income stays the same, then that income will not buy as many goods and services. The person will be worse off.

4. When most (not all) prices are rising in the economy, people can be hurt if their incomes are not going up as fast as or faster than prices. **Inflation** is a rise in the average price level. Inflation reduces the value of money; that is, a dollar cannot purchase as many goods and services. If an economy is experiencing inflation, it means that, on average, prices are rising. Some prices may be falling, but not enough to offset the rise in other prices.

5. Explain that most people know when their incomes increase, and they know by how much their incomes increase, i. e., the percent change. Read the following scenario.

   Suppose Andie was earning $4.00 per hour baby-sitting, but she now earns $4.25 per hour. Her hourly wage increased by 6.25%. Andie buys many different goods and services such as soft drinks, hamburgers and fries, candy bars, movie tickets, and clothes.

6. Ask whether Andie is better or worse off? (We don't know because we don't know whether prices have gone up, gone down, or stayed the same.)

   Discuss the following:
   a. If people's incomes don't rise when inflation increases, what happens to their purchasing power? (It falls.)
   b. What does this mean? (People are able to buy fewer goods and services with the same amount of income.)
   c. Dan's income rises 3 percent and inflation is 4 percent. Is Dan better or worse off? Why? (Dan is worse off because prices are going up faster than his income. He won't be able to buy as many goods and services as before. His purchasing power has declined.)
   d. Cara's income rises 5 percent and inflation is 4 percent. Is Cara better or worse off? Why? (Cara is better off because her income is increasing faster than prices, so she'll be able to buy more goods and services than before. Her purchasing power has increased.)
   e. Pedro's income rises 4 percent and inflation is 4 percent. Is Pedro better or worse off? Why? (Pedro is neither better nor worse off. He can buy the same amount of goods and services because his income increase matches the increase in prices. His purchasing power is the same.)

7. Explain that the **Consumer Price Index** (CPI) is a tool used to measure changes in the prices of most goods and services that people buy. By knowing about and understanding the CPI, people can analyze the impact of a wage change on their purchasing power. People can determine whether their purchasing power is increasing, decreasing, or staying the same.

8. Explain that an **index** is a number derived from a formula used to characterize a set of data. Point out that one way to measure changes in the overall price level is to calculate a price index. A **price index** shows how much the average price of a group of goods and services has changed over time.

9. Explain that to develop a price index, experts identify a combination of goods and services representing what most people buy. This combination of goods and services is often referred to as a **market basket**.

10. Point out that movie tickets, 12-ounce cans of soft drinks, hamburgers and fries, and candy bars comprise a group of goods and services that middle-school students may buy. This group of goods and services will represent the students' market basket. After experts identify a market basket, they collect data and use the data to construct an index based on the changes in the prices of these goods. Display Visual 4.2 and use the example to explain how a price index is calculated.

11. Have the students calculate the percent change in the market basket price from year to year. (During year 2, the change is 26.4%. During year 3, the change is 21.7%.)

    Explain that the percent change in the overall price level from one year to another is called the **rate of inflation**. The inflation rate is stated as a percentage. For year 2 the inflation rate is 26.4% and for year 3 it is 21.7%. Have the students look at the sample price index at the bottom of Visual 4.2. Note that the percent change in the index from year 1 to year 2 is also 26.4 (*[(126.4 – 100)/100] x 100*), which is the inflation rate for that year. Have the students calculate the inflation rate for year 3 using the price index.

    [153.8 – 126.4]/126.4] x 100 = 21.7 or 21.7%

12. Discuss the following.
    a. What data does this index represent? (A set of goods, quantities, and prices for three different years.)
    b. In this example, year 1 is designated as the "base" year. What does that mean? (The starting year to which other years are compared.)

c. What's the difference between "inflation" and "rate of inflation"?

(Inflation means that most prices are going up. The rate of inflation indicates how much prices are increasing compared to another time.)

Optional Questions

d. How would the inflation rate change from year to year if two movie tickets were included in the market basket instead of one?

(In year two, the inflation rate would be [10.70 – 8.30)/8.30] × 100 = 28.9%. In year 3, the inflation rate would be [(13.15 – 10.70)/10.70] × 100 = 22.9%.)

e. Why does the rate of inflation increase when the number of movie tickets purchased increases?

(Movie tickets account for a large portion of the market basket. The price of a movie ticket has increased 50%, so it has a higher impact on the rate of inflation, pulling the inflation rate above 28.9% in year two. NOTE: The inflation rates in this example are higher than typically occur in the United States. Students are much more likely to read about inflation rates of 2-6% in the next few years.)

13. Remind the students that whether people are better or worse off because of inflation depends on whether their incomes rose faster or slower than the prices of the things they buy. For the sample price index, students must know how wages changed over time to determine whether people were better or worse off (that is, had more or less purchasing power).

14. Tell the students that they will visit a website where they can learn what prices and wages today equaled in another year. A **nominal price** is one expressed in today's dollars. The website adjusts the price for inflation over time. This adjusted price is referred to as a **real price**.

15. Explain that the website bases its calculations on the Consumer Price Index (CPI)—the price index most often used to measure inflation. The Bureau of Labor Statistics (BLS) computes it each month. The BLS uses a group of goods or market basket that is purchased monthly by the "typical" urban consumer, just as the class used a group of goods in its calculation of a price index.

16. Display Visual 4.3. Explain that this is the Consumer Price Index from 1975 to 2000. Point out that the index numbers increase every year, and ask what the increasing numbers indicate. (Inflation.) However, the index does not tell the reader the annual rate of inflation.

17. Display Visual 4.2 to review the process for calculating the annual rate of inflation. Use the information from Visual 4.3 to calculate the annual rate of inflation for a year.

18. Distribute a copy of Visual 4.3 to each student, and tell them to compute the annual rate of inflation for the remaining years as a homework assignment.

19. Divide the class into groups of 2-3 students, and distribute a copy of Activity 4.1. Allow the students to visit *www.minneapolisfed.org/ economy/calc/cpihome.html*. Explain that they should begin with 2000, enter wages and prices, have the calculator convert the price they enter to 1945 prices, and record the answers they receive in the blank table on Activity 4.1. Note: If you do not have Internet access, display Visual 4.5. The table on this visual has the movie ticket prices and baby-sitting wages converted.

20. Discuss the following.
    a. What is the definition of nominal price? (The current price.) Real price? (A price adjusted for inflation.)
    b. What is the definition of nominal wage (income)? (The current wage or income.) **Real wage (income)**? (The wage or income adjusted for inflation.)
    c. What was the nominal baby-sitting price (wage) in 2000? ($4.00)
    d. What was the 2000 real price received by a baby-sitter in 1945 terms? ($.42)
    e. What was the nominal price of a movie in 2000? ($6.00)
    f. What was the real price of a 2000 movie ticket in 1945 terms? ($.63)
    g. Was a movie ticket relatively cheaper in 2000 or in the good old days of 1945? (In 1945, a baby-sitter had to baby-sit for one and 1/4 hour to buy a movie ticket. In 2000, a baby-sitter had to baby-sit one and one-half hours to buy a movie ticket. Movies were relatively cheaper in 1945—the good old days.)
    h. Do you think that's always true? (Probably not. It depends on how much a person earned, what that person bought, and the relative prices.)

21. Distribute two sheets of graph paper and two colored pencils to each student. Tell the students to use one sheet of graph paper and the data they entered in Activity 4.1 to construct scatter plots and lines of best fit for nominal movie ticket prices and real movie ticket prices. They should use the other sheet of graph paper to construct scatter plots and lines of best fit for nominal baby-sitting wages and real baby-sitting wages. Have the students compare the slopes of the lines.

Optional: Allow time for the students to use the CPI calculator to convert wages of athletes, movie stars, and politicians and/or the costs and revenues from movies over time to a base year for comparison.

Optional: Have the students do some research on the CPI to learn more about what goods and services are included in the market basket and how the data are collected by the BLS.

Closure

Review the main points of the lesson by asking the following questions.

a. What is the purchasing power of a person's income? (The amount of goods and services the person can buy.)
b. What happens to purchasing power if prices rise and wages don't rise? (Decreases.)
c. What happens to purchasing power if prices rise and wages rise by the same amount? (Remains the same.)
d. What is inflation? (A rise in the average price level.)
e. How can inflation be measured? (Price indexes.)
f. What is an index? (A number derived from a formula used to characterize a set of data.)
g. What is a price index? (A number derived to describe the average price of a group or market basket of goods.)
h. What is the rate of inflation? (Rate of inflation is the percent change in the overall price level from one year to another.)
i. Which price index is most commonly used? (Consumer Price Index)
j. What do we mean by nominal? (A value stated in today's or current prices.)
k. What do we mean by real prices or wages? (Prices or wages adjusted for inflation.)
l. If we want to compare prices and wages in one year to prices and wages in another year, what must we do? (Adjust them for inflation by converting nominal prices and wages to real prices and wages.)

ACTIVITY 4.1 ▲ Really, What Is the Price?

Instructions:

▶ Go to www.minneapolisfed.org/economy/calc/cpihome.html and use the CPI calculator to complete the following table.

▶ Adjust the baby-sitting prices (wages) to 1945 prices in column 1.

▶ Adjust the movie ticket prices to 1945 prices in column 5.

Example for 1980 baby-sitting prices:

If in 1980 I bought goods or services for $ 2.00

in 1945 the same goods or services would cost $ .44

The 1945 price of $.44 appears after you hit the "calculate" button.

1	2	3	4	5
Real Baby-sitting Price (Wage) Per Hour Adjusted to 1945 Prices	Nominal Baby-sitting Price (Wage) Per Hour	Year	Nominal Movie Ticket Prices	Real Movie Ticket Prices Adjusted to 1945 Prices
	$.20	1945	$.25	
	.35	1950	.60	
	.40	1955	.75	
	.50	1960	1.00	
	.60	1965	1.25	
	.90	1970	1.75	
	1.50	1975	2.50	
	2.00	1980	3.00	
	2.50	1985	3.25	
	2.75	1990	5.00	
	3.00	1995	5.50	
	4.00	2000	6.00	

VISUAL 4.1

Baby-sitting Price (Wage) Per Hour	Year	Movie Ticket Prices
$ .20	1945	$ .25
.35	1950	.60
.40	1955	.75
.50	1960	1.00
.60	1965	1.25
.90	1970	1.75
1.50	1975	2.50
2.00	1980	3.00
2.50	1985	3.25
2.75	1990	5.00
3.00	1995	5.50
4.00	2000	6.00

VISUAL 4.2 ▲ Calculating a Price Index

Good/Service	Amount Bought	Price in Year 1	Price in Year 2	Price in Year 3
Movie ticket	1	3.00	4.00	5.00
12 oz. can of soda	2	.40	.45	.55
Hamburger and fries	1	1.00	1.10	1.35
Candy bar (1.05 oz.)	2	.25	.35	.35
TOTAL		5.30	6.70	8.15

Market Basket = 1 movie ticket, 2 cans of soda, 1 hamburger and fries, and 2 candy bars

Market Basket in year 1 = (1 x 3.00) + (2 x .40) + (1 x 1.00) + (2 x .25) = 5.30

Market Basket in year 2 = (1 x 4.00) + (2 x .45) + (1 x 1.10) + (2 x .35) = 6.70

Market Basket in year 3 = (1 x 5.00) + (2 x .55) + (1 x 1.35) + (2 x .35) = 8.15

A price index has a base year to which prices in all other years are compared.

Assume that year 1 is the base year.

Price index = (market basket price in a given year / market price in the base year) x 100

So, the price index for the base year is (5.30/5.30) x 100 = 1 x 100 = 100

The price index for year 2 is (6.70/5.30) x 100 = 126.4

The price index for year 3 is (8.15/5.30) x 100 = 153.8

Sample Price Index

Annual Indexes	
Year 1	100.0
Year 2	126.4
Year 3	153.8

The percent change in the overall price level from one year to another is called the **rate of inflation**. The inflation rate is stated as a percentage.

Year 2:
The inflation rate is 26.4%, calculated as follows:
[(126.4 − 100)/100] x 100 = 26.4%

Year 3:
The inflation rate is 21.7%, calculated as follows:
[(153.8 − 126.4)/126.4] x 100 = 21.7%

VISUAL 4.3 ▲ The Consumer Price Index, 1975–2000

Annual Indexes		Inflation Rate
1975	53.8	
1976	56.9	
1977	60.6	
1978	65.2	
1979	72.6	
1980	82.4	
1981	90.9	
1982	96.5	
1983	99.6	
1984	103.9	
1985	107.6	
1986	109.6	
1987	113.6	
1988	118.3	
1989	124.0	
1990	130.7	
1991	136.2	
1992	140.3	
1993	144.5	
1994	148.2	
1995	152.4	
1996	156.9	
1997	160.5	
1998	163.0	
1999	166.6	
2000	172.2	

Source: U.S. Department of Labor, Bureau of Labor Statistics.

The Consumer Price Index, 1975–2000

Annual Indexes		Inflation Rate
1975	53.8	Not applicable
1976	56.9	5.8%
1977	60.6	6.5%
1978	65.2	7.6%
1979	72.6	11.3%
1980	82.4	13.5%
1981	90.9	10.3%
1982	96.5	6.2%
1983	99.6	3.2%
1984	103.9	4.3%
1985	107.6	3.6%
1986	109.6	1.9%
1987	113.6	3.6%
1988	118.3	4.1%
1989	124.0	4.8%
1990	130.7	5.4%
1991	136.2	4.2%
1992	140.3	3.0%
1993	144.5	3.0%
1994	148.2	2.6%
1995	152.4	2.8%
1996	156.9	3.0%
1997	160.5	2.3%
1998	163.0	1.6%
1999	166.6	2.2%
2000	172.2	3.4%

Source: U.S. Department of Labor, Bureau of Labor Statistics.

VISUAL 4.5 ▲ Answers to Activity 4.1

1	2	3	4	5
Real Baby-sitting Price (Wage) Per Hour Adjusted to 1945 Prices	Nominal Baby-sitting Price (Wage) Per Hour	Year	Nominal Movie Ticket Prices	Real Movie Ticket Prices Adjusted to 1945 Prices
.20	$.20	1945	$.25	.25
.26	.35	1950	.60	.45
.27	.40	1955	.75	.50
.30	.50	1960	1.00	.61
.34	.60	1965	1.25	.71
.42	.90	1970	1.75	.81
.50	1.50	1975	2.50	.84
.44	2.00	1980	3.00	.66
.42	2.50	1985	3.25	.54
.38	2.75	1990	5.00	.69
.35	3.00	1995	5.50	.65
.42	4.00	2000	6.00	.63

Why Is Everyone So Crazy About Cell Phones?

Mathematics Prerequisites

Prior to this lesson, students should know:
- A ratio compares two quantities.
- A proportion states that two ratios are equivalent.

Lesson Objectives

Students will be able to:
- Define *competition*.
- Calculate and compare differing rates for cell phone services.
- Organize and analyze data on cell phone services.
- Make conjectures about the correlation between price and service and the number of competitors in the marketplace.

Abstract

This lesson is designed to introduce students to the benefits of competition utilizing proportions to compare different rates. The students will explore the market for cell phones in two activities. In activity one, the students are asked to solve for the unit rate of several cell phone providers and draw conclusions about the relative prices. In activity two, the students take on the role of a cell phone service provider and put together a monthly plan to sell to customers. The lesson concludes with the students graphing the unit rates for cell phone airtime over several periods and summarizing their findings.

Mathematics Terms

- Whole number operations
- Rates
- Proportions

Materials

- One copy of Activities 5.1 and 5.2 for each pair of students in the class
- Transparency of Visual 5.1 and one copy for each pair of students
- One *Cell Phone Provider Card* (for each group of two students)
- Transparencies of Visual 5.2 and 5.3

Estimated Time

One class period

Warm-Up Activity

Many problems can be solved using a proportion. By changing a ratio to a unit rate we can find values for any amount of items. For example, if we know our car traveled 360 miles and used 15 gallons of gas, the ratio of miles to gallon or 360/15 can be simplified to the unit rate of 24 miles per gallon by dividing 360 by 15. We can use this to plan how much gas it will require to travel any number of miles, or how many miles we can travel on a given amount of gas. We can also use it to compare one vehicle with other vehicles. Solve the following problems:

1. If you can buy oranges at $3.25 for 5 pounds, find the unit rate price per pound and use that information to find the price for 12 pounds. ($7.80.)

2. You quizzed 10 classmates and found that the number of TVs in all 10 households was 28.
   a. Write this as a ratio of TVs to households (28/10)
   b. Find the unit rate of TVs per household (2.8/1)
   c. Use this information to predict the number of TVs in 365 households. (1,022 TVs.)

Procedures

1. Bring a cell phone with you to class and immediately following taking attendance, have the phone begin ringing. Note: if there is a cell phone ban in your school, make sure to inform the administration of your intent to use the phone, briefly, for instructional purposes. Allow the phone to ring enough to attract the attention of the entire class. Answer the phone and hold a quick conversation, something regarding the quality of students currently in class or how important the understanding of mathematics is for future success. Something to generate a small laugh from the group or a collective rolling of their eyes, as if to say, "Yeah-right." End the conversation and power down the phone. Discuss the following:
   a. So, are you surprised I actually own and operate a cell phone? (Responses will vary.) I have actually had this phone for about one year. (Or substitute in your own information.) Do any of you have your own cell phone? (Count and record on the board the number of students with their own phones.) Do any of your friends own a cell phone? (Count and record, on the board, the number of students with friends who own cell phones.) Do any of your families own a cell phone? (Count and record the number on the board.)
   b. Well, looking at the numbers on the board, it is pretty surprising how many people own cell phones. Why do you suppose so many of our friends and families own cell phones? Let's make a list of some of the benefits you think are important in owning a cell

phone. (Write the word "Benefit" on the board and record student responses.)

   c. Let's divide up into pairs for an activity on cell phones. Your job will be to determine why cell phones have become such a common device. After all, just a few years ago hardly anyone owned a cell phone.

2. Distribute one copy of Visual 5.1 to each pair of students. Display Visual 5.1 on the overhead. Briefly review the information. You may want to comment on the use of the word "Period." This designates a point in time. The periods are equal in length. Notice that the number of firms providing cell phone service is increasing over time.

3. Divide the class into groups of two students per group. Distribute Activity 5.1. The students will calculate the different prices per minute of talk time and draw conclusions about why cell phones have become a common device. Review the instructions on the activity. Allow approximately 15 minutes for the students to complete Activity 5.1.

4. Call the groups back together to discuss the activity. Review the answers to each question on Activity 5.1. Discuss the following:

   We have just calculated the rates for different providers and have seen that these rates change over time. In this next activity you and your partner will draw a card that places you in one of the four time periods. Your job will be to select a name for your company and then set up a cell phone package to compete for customers in your period.

5. Distribute one Cell Phone Provider Card to each pair of students. Allow approximately 5 minutes to complete the instructions on the card.

6. On the board, create four columns labeled "Period 1." "Period 2," "Period 3," Period 4." Call the groups back together and discuss the following:

   a. Now that you have completed your cards, I am curious about the cell phone plans you set up for your firm. I would like a representative from each group to come up to the board and record your package information in the appropriate column. Be sure to include your company name.

   b. Looking at the data on the board, I see quite a bit of difference in the pricing and service of these plans. What criterion or guideline did you use to decide what to offer in your plan? (The responses will vary but should follow the general rule that price and services were based on what others in the market were offering. Also, each card had some restrictions regarding the providers' own prices that students were not to price below. These restrictions represent a break-even point for the provider.)

   c. What do you suppose would happen if I took one of the plans (select a plan from Period 1 and refer to it by name) from Period 1 and put it in Period 4? (No one would purchase the plan.) **Why would people avoid buying airtime from "Name of the provider"?** (Everyone can buy airtime cheaper from one of the other providers.)

d. **As a customer, in which period would you like to be in the position to buy cell phone airtime?** (Period 4.) **Why?** (Prices are less expensive.)

e. **Looking at the different periods, what change do you see in the services provided by the various providers?** (Services have increased over time.)

f. **Why do you suppose that price and services have improved over time?** (An increase in the number of providers.)

g. **How does the number of providers make a difference in the price of owning a cell phone?** (Competition.)

h. **Competition is the key word here. (Write the word "Competition" on the board.) Competition means that providers must try to win your business by offering better prices and services.**

i. **Excellent work everyone. I would now like you, individually, to graph the information we have been discussing today and provide a conclusion about why cell phones are so popular.**

7. Distribute Activity 5.2. Review the instructions. Depending on the amount of time left in the class period, Activity 5.2 may be assigned as homework.

Extension

1. Assign the students the task of finding cell phone plans in the local newspaper and bringing them to class for discussion.

2. Ask the students to research their own family's cell phone plan and complete a summary to submit as an assignment. The various packages could be discussed and the rates compared for the entire class.

ACTIVITY 5.1 ▲ Cell Phones in Henley

The information contained in Activity 5.1 represents the market for cell phones in the town of Henley. The data is organized by periods. Each period represents an equal length of time. A cell phone service provider is a firm that offers cell phones, airtime, and additional services. The purchase of a cell phone represents a one-time-only charge when a customer signs on with a provider. Other services are packaged and sold for a monthly fee. With a partner, answer the questions below.

1. How many periods are listed on Visual 5.1?_____

2. Write the names of each provider in the space provided below.

   a. _____

   b. _____

   c. _____

   d. _____

3. In which period did **All-Talk** begin offering a cell phone package in Henley?_____

4. Which provider has offered a cell phone package in each of the four periods?_____

5. Which provider was the last to enter the cell phone market in Henley?_____

You and your partner will now compare the rates and services offered by the cell phone providers for each time period. Your comparison will be based on the price of a phone, the price of airtime, and the additional services offered by each firm.

6. For Period 1, calculate the price per minute of airtime using the proportion below:

Period 1	
$150/100 minutes = $X/1minute	
Blue Sky	Price per Minute = _____

7. In Period 2, we see that a new firm has entered the market. Using two proportions, calculate the price per minute of airtime for both firms and record below.

Period 2	
All-Talk	Price per Minute = _____
Blue Sky	Price per Minute = _____

Which firm has the lowest rate? _____

8. In Period 3, we see that another new firm has entered the market. Using proportions, calculate the price per minute of airtime for all three firms and record below.

Period 3	
Com-Quest	Price per Minute = _____
All-Talk	Price per Minute = _____
Blue Sky	Price per Minute = _____

Which firm has the lowest rate? _____

9. In Period 4, there are a total of four firms in the cell phone market. Using proportions, calculate the price per minute of airtime for all four firms and record below.

Period 4	
Max-Chat	Price per Minute = _____
Com-Quest	Price per Minute = _____
All-Talk	Price per Minute = _____
Blue Sky	Price per Minute = _____

Which firm has the lowest rate? _____

10. Each firm requires new customers to purchase a phone when signing up for cell phone service. Using the chart below, calculate the average price of a cell phone for each of the four periods.

Average Price of a Cell Phone in Periods 1-4	
Period 1	Average Price = _____
Period 2	Average Price = _____
Period 3	Average Price = _____
Period 4	Average Price = _____

ACTIVITY 5.1 (continued)

11. Describe the change in the price of a cell phone over time._____

12. Each firm in the Henley cell phone market also began offering voice mail service to its customers. Using the chart below, calculate the average price for voice mail service for each of the four periods.

Average Price of Voice Mail Service in Periods 1-4	
Period 1	Average Price = _____
Period 2	Average Price = _____
Period 3	Average Price = _____
Period 4	Average Price = _____

13. Describe the change in price for voice mail service over time._____

ACTIVITY 5.2

1. Using the information you calculated in Activity 5.1, complete the chart below:

Period	Number of Providers	Average Price per Minute of Airtime
1		
2		
3		
4		

2. Using the summary information from the chart above, graph, as ordered pairs, Number of Cell Phone Providers on the horizontal axis and Average Price per Minute on the vertical axis.

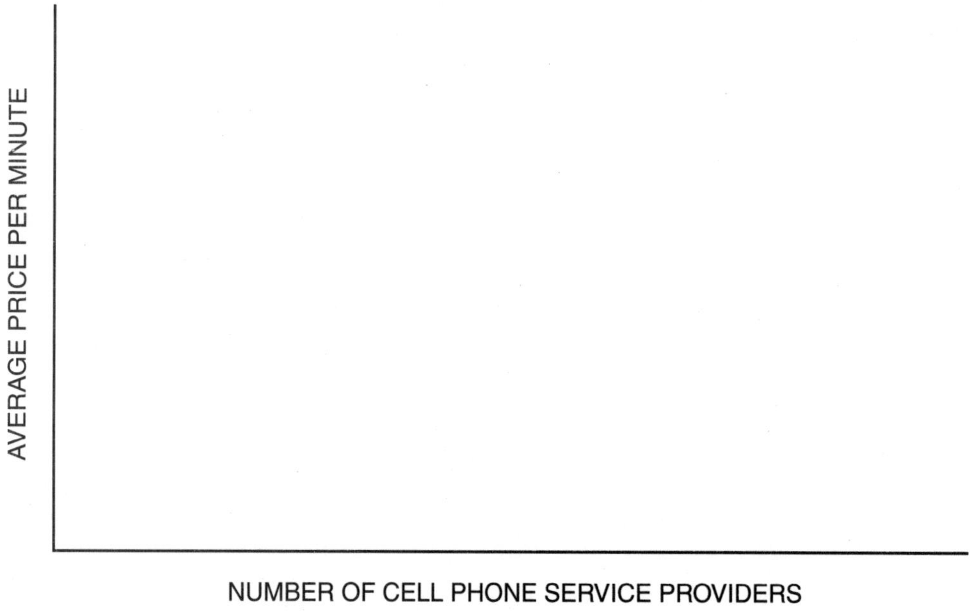

AVERAGE PRICE PER MINUTE

NUMBER OF CELL PHONE SERVICE PROVIDERS

3. Describe the relationship between average price per minute of airtime and the number of cell phone service providers.

4. How has competition between providers affected the price of using a cell phone?

5. What could you predict will happen to the prices of cell phone services in Period 5?

6. How does competition benefit people?

VISUAL 5.1 ▲ Cell Phone Service Providers

By Period

Period 1	Period 2	Period 3	Period 4
Provider: **Blue Sky** Price-$150 per month Includes 100 minutes of airtime Price of phone-$300 No Additional Services Provided	Provider: **All-Talk** Price-$125 per month Includes 150 minutes of airtime Price of phone-$200 Price of Voice Mail: $10 per month	Provider: **Com-Quest** Price-$100 per month Includes 250 minutes of airtime Price of phone-$100 Price of Voice Mail: $5 per month	Provider: **Max-Chat** Price-$75 per month Includes 300 minutes of airtime Free Phone Free Voice Mail Free Call Waiting
	Provider: **Blue Sky** Price-$125 per month Includes 100 minutes of airtime Price of phone-$200 Price of Voice Mail: $15 per month	Provider: **All-Talk** Price-$100 per month Includes 200 minutes of airtime Price of phone-$100 Price of Voice Mail: $5 per month	Provider: **Com-Quest** Price-$75 per month Includes 250 minutes of airtime Price of phone-$50 Free Voice-Mail
		Provider: **Blue Sky** Price-$100 per month Includes 160 minutes of airtime Price of phone-$100 Price of Voice Mail: $5 per month	Provider: **All-Talk** Price-$50 per month Includes 200 minutes of airtime Free Phone Price of Voice Mail: $5 per month
			Provider: **Blue Sky** Price-$45 per month Includes 150 minutes of airtime Price of phone-$30 Price of Voice Mail: $10 per month

VISUAL 5.2 ▲ Answers to Activity 5.1

The information contained in Activity 5.1 represents the market for cell phones in the town of Henley. The data is organized by periods. Each period represents an equal length of time. A cell phone service provider is a firm that offers cell phones, airtime, and additional services. The purchase of a cell phone represents a one-time-only charge when a customer signs on with a provider. Other services are packaged and sold for a monthly fee. With a partner, answer the questions below.

1. How many periods are listed on Handout 5.1? 4

2. Write the names of each provider in the space provided below.
   a. Blue Sky
   b. All-Talk
   c. Com-Quest
   d. Max-Chat

3. In which period did **All-Talk** begin offering a cell phone package in Henley? Period 2

4. Which provider has offered a cell phone package in each of the four periods? Blue Sky

5. Which provider was the last to enter the cell phone market in Henley? Max-Chat

You and your partner will now compare the rates and services offered by the cell phone providers for each time period. Your comparison will be based on the price of a phone, the price of airtime, and the additional services offered by each firm.

6. For Period 1, calculate the price per minute of airtime using the proportion below:

Period 1	
$150/100 minutes = $X/1minute	
Blue Sky	Price per Minute = $1.50

7. In Period 2, we see that a new firm has entered the market. Using two proportions, calculate the price per minute of airtime for both firms and record below.

Period 2	
All-Talk	Price per Minute = $.83
Blue Sky	Price per Minute = $1.25

Which firm has the lowest rate? All-Talk

8. In Period 3, we see that another new firm has entered the market. Using proportions, calculate the price per minute of airtime for all three firms and record below.

Period 3	
Com-Quest	Price per Minute = $.40
All-Talk	Price per Minute = $.50
Blue Sky	Price per Minute = $.625

Which firm has the lowest rate? Com-Quest

9. In Period 4, there are a total of four firms in the cell phone market. Using proportions, calculate the price per minute of airtime for all four firms and record below.

Period 4	
Max-Chat	Price per Minute = $.25
Com-Quest	Price per Minute = $.30
All-Talk	Price per Minute = $.25
Blue Sky	Price per Minute = $.30

Which firm has the lowest rate? Max-Chat and All-Talk

10. Each firm requires new customers to purchase a phone when signing up for cell phone service. Using the chart below, calculate the average price of a cell phone for each of the four periods.

Average Price of a Cell Phone in Periods 1-4	
Period 1	Average Price = $300
Period 2	Average Price = $200
Period 3	Average Price = $100
Period 4	Average Price = $20

11. Describe the change in the price of a cell phone over time. It decreased.

12. Each firm in the Henley cell phone market also began offering voice mail service to its customers. Using the chart below, calculate the average price for voice mail service for each of the four periods.

Average Price of Voice Mail Service in Periods 1-4	
Period 1	Average Price = Not available
Period 2	Average Price = $12.50
Period 3	Average Price = $5.00
Period 4	Average Price = $3.75

13. Describe the change in price for voice mail service over time. The price for voice mail was reduced over time.

VISUAL 5.3 ▲ Answers to Activity 5.2

1. Using the information you calculated in Activity 5.1, complete the chart below:

Period	Number of Providers	Average Price per Minute of Airtime
1	1	$ 1.50
2	2	$1.04
3	3	$.51
4	4	$.28

2. Using the summary information from the chart above, graph, as ordered pairs, Number of Cell Phone Providers on the horizontal axis and Average Price per Minute on the vertical axis.

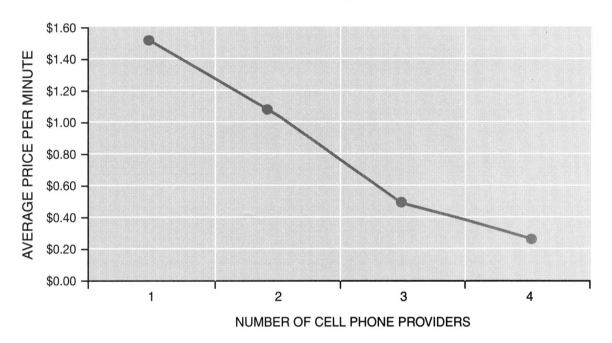

NUMBER OF CELL PHONE PROVIDERS

3. Describe the relationship between average price per minute of airtime and the number of cell phone service providers.

As the number of providers increased, the average price per minute of airtime decreased; an inverse relationship exists between number of providers and average price per minute of airtime.

4. How has competition between providers affected the price of using a cell phone?

The price that people pay to use a cell phone, buy a cell phone and the use of voice-mail, were all reduced.

VISUAL 5.3 (continued)

5. What could you predict will happen to the prices of cell phone services in Period 5?

   Prices could continue to decrease as providers compete for customers. If additional providers enter the market, prices will continue to fall.

6. How does competition benefit people?

   Competition in the market for cell phones added services and reduced prices for people using cell phones.

Cell Phone Provider Cards

Period 1 Provider	**Period 2 Provider**	**Period 3 Provider**	**Period 4 Provider**
You are a new cell phone provider entering the market in Period 1. You must compete for customers against the other firms in the market. Complete the following tasks and record your information on the back of this card. 1. Select a name for your firm. 2. Set a monthly fee for airtime. You may not charge less than $1.35 per minute. 3. Select a price for the phone. You many not charge less than $275. 4. Select a voice mail option to offer customers. You many not charge less than $20 per month.	You are a new cell phone provider entering the market in Period 2. You must compete for customers against the other firms in the market. Complete the following tasks and record your information on the back of this card. 1. Select a name for your firm. 2. Set a monthly fee for airtime. You may not charge less than $.75 per minute. 3. Select a price for the phone. You many not charge less than $190. 4. Select a voice mail option to offer customers. You many not charge less than $10 per month.	You are a new cell phone provider entering the market in Period 3. You must compete for customers against the other firms in the market. Complete the following tasks and record your information on the back of this card. 1. Select a name for your firm. 2. Set a monthly fee for airtime. You may not charge less than $.35 per minute. 3. Select a price for the phone. You many not charge less than $100. 4. Select a voice mail option to offer customers. You many not charge less than $5 per month.	You are a new cell phone provider entering the market in Period 4. You must compete for customers against the other firms in the market. Complete the following tasks and record your information on the back of this card. 1. Select a name for your firm. 2. Set a monthly fee for airtime. You may not charge less than $.20 per minute and you can offer a $10 rebate to anyone selecting to use your service. 3. Select a price for the phone. You may provide the phone for free. 4. Select a voice mail option to offer customers. You many not charge less than $5 per month.
Period 1 Provider	**Period 2 Provider**	**Period 3 Provider**	**Period 4 Provider**
You are a new cell phone provider entering the market in Period 1. You must compete for customers against the other firms in the market. Complete the following tasks and record your information on the back of this card. 1. Select a name for your firm. 2. Set a monthly fee for airtime. You may not charge less than $1.35 per minute. 3. Select a price for the phone. You many not charge less than $275. 4. Select a voice mail option to offer customers. You many not charge less than $20 per month.	You are a new cell phone provider entering the market in Period 2. You must compete for customers against the other firms in the market. Complete the following tasks and record your information on the back of this card. 1. Select a name for your firm. 2. Set a monthly fee for airtime. You may not charge less than $.75 per minute. 3. Select a price for the phone. You many not charge less than $190. 4. Select a voice mail option to offer customers. You many not charge less than $10 per month.	You are a new cell phone provider entering the market in Period 3. You must compete for customers against the other firms in the market. Complete the following tasks and record your information on the back of this card. 1. Select a name for your firm. 2. Set a monthly fee for airtime. You may not charge less than $.35 per minute. 3. Select a price for the phone. You many not charge less than $100. 4. Select a voice mail option to offer customers. You many not charge less than $5 per month.	You are a new cell phone provider entering the market in Period 4. You must compete for customers against the other firms in the market. Complete the following tasks and record your information on the back of this card. 1. Select a name for your firm. 2. Set a monthly fee for airtime. You may not charge less than $.20 per minute and you can offer a $10 rebate to anyone selecting to use your service. 3. Select a price for the phone. You may provide the phone for free. 4. Select a voice mail option to offer customers. You many not charge less than $5 per month.

How Much is That Bike?

Mathematics Prerequisites

Prior to this lesson, students should know:
> Multiplication.
> Percents.

Lesson Objectives

Students will be able to:
> Define *percent, principal, interest, rate of interest, cost,* and *benefit.*
> Explain the advantages of using percents in comparing numbers of unequal size.
> Calculate the additional costs of using credit to make a purchase.
> Compare the costs and benefits of purchasing a bike on credit.

Abstract

This lesson demonstrates the utility of percentages in comparing fractions of unequal size; it also provides students with practice in using percent to calculate simple interest. Students are introduced to the idea of buying on credit and the additional resources required to service the debt. The concept of costs and benefits is examined as students compare the additional costs of borrowing money to purchase the bike versus the additional benefits of getting the bike right now.

Mathematics Terms

> Multiplication
> Decimals
> Percents

Materials

> Fraction Cards: one for each student. (Each fraction card has a "front" and "back." The "fronts" are different for each student, but the "backs" are the same. You'll need to staple or paste the "fronts" to the "backs.")
> One copy of Activity 6.1 and 6.2 for each student
> Transparencies of Visuals 6.1–6.3

Estimated Time

One class period

Warm-Up

Three girl scouts, Bee, Lee, Dee, participated in the annual sale of Girl Scout cookies. Bee sold 54 boxes, which is 75% of the number of boxes she started with. Dee sold 45 of the 50 boxes she started with. Lee sold 2/3 of the 96 boxes she started with.

a. Who sold the most boxes? How many? (Lee sold the most boxes, since 2/3 of 96 is 64 boxes.)

b. Who sold the greatest percent of the number she started with? What percent? (Dee sold the greatest percent. 45 of 50 is 90% of her boxes. Bee sold 75%, and Lee's 2/3 represents about 67%.)

Procedures

1. Students will work in groups of three for the first activity. To set up the groups, distribute one Fraction Card to each student. Each Fraction Card has a fraction on the front and directions on the back. This grouping is based on equivalent fractions and group size of three. Students must find partners based on who else in the room has the same fraction. As an example, a group of three might have Fraction Cards of 14/16, 21/24, and 28/32, all of which reduce to 7/8. Once the students find their equivalents, they are instructed to sit together and discuss Step 2 on their Fraction Card.

2. Instruct the students to push all the desks out from the center of the room; distribute one Fraction Card to each student. Announce that each student is to find his or her other two partners based on the fraction listed on the card. Allow approximately 5 minutes for this grouping; then call the groups to attention and discuss the following:

a. Who can report on how the groups in this room have been formed? (The same fraction, a reduced fraction, fractions in their lowest common denominator.)

b. What method did you use to find the lowest common denominator? (Reduced, set up equivalent proportions.)

c. How did you know if someone did not belong in your group? (The fraction was not the same; the fraction did not reduce to the same lowest common denominator.)

d. What we did in the grouping process was have you decide if someone had a fraction that was similar to or different from your own number. It might be interesting to see if you can arrange all the factions in this room from the smallest to the largest; let's see how quickly you can complete the task.

e. On your Fraction Card you will find the letter A, B, or C. I am going to ask you to regroup based on the letter on your card. Each of the new groups will have someone representing each fraction. Within the A, B, and C groups, you will arrange yourselves in order from the smallest to the largest fraction and complete this task in two minutes. Once you have decided on the order of your fractions, sit down on the floor to indicate you are satisfied with the arrangement.

f. A's report to the back of the room, B's to the front of the room, and C's to the center of the room. You may begin arranging yourselves right now. (Prepare for chaos as the groups try to determine the most efficient method to organize themselves. You may offer assistance to a group or individual who may struggle with the activity.)

3. Allow only two minutes for the activity. Once the two minutes are up, call the class to attention and discuss the following:

a. Everyone please face the front of the room. Does any group believe that they are absolutely correct in their arrangement? (Note which groups believe they are correct although it is unlikely that they managed to correctly distribute themselves in just two minutes.)

b. How did your group do? Group A, did you find the correct order? Group B? Group C? Why do you suppose it was so difficult to discover the correct order? (Not enough time, no common way to compare fractions of unequal size, etc.)

c. Does anyone have a suggestion on how we could complete the ordering task within the two-minute time limit? (Answers will vary, but we are looking for a response that would make all the fractions equivalent; then it would be much easier to compare.)

d. How about if we were able to complete a simple calculation that would make it possible to compare all the fractions within your group? If we are going to make the comparison, we will need all the fractions to have an equivalent base on which to compare. Right now we have 4ths, 5ths, 8ths, 10ths, and 20ths. To make this comparison we will convert each fraction to 100ths, using a simple proportion.

e. As an example, let's convert 18/25 to 100ths. (On the board write the proportion below.) If we cross multiple, we find that $1,800 = (x)(25)$ and if we solve for x, we find that 18/25 is equivalent to 72/100.

$$\frac{18}{25} = \frac{x}{100}$$

f. I would like each of you now to convert your fraction to 100ths, using proportions as I just demonstrated on the board. (Allow several minutes to complete this task.)

g. Now that everyone has his or her fraction in 100ths, do you think we can arrange the fractions in order from largest to smallest? Well, let's give it a try. Everyone stand up and within your group of A, or B, or C you will have two minutes to arrange your group in order. Remember to sit down in order once your group is set on the arrangement. Everyone ready? You may begin now. (Allow exactly two minutes for the arrangement.)

h. Time is up, everyone please sit down, if you haven't already done so. Well, does any group feel they are in the exact order from smallest to largest? (Acknowledge those groups that believe they are correct and display Visual 6.1.)

i. Congratulations to everyone for your efforts in arranging these fractions in their proper order. Did you know that in a study conducted a few years ago, over 2/3 of the middle school students tested could not compare and correctly order fractions? Isn't that amazing, and you guys completed the task, the second time so easily. Why do you suppose it was so much easier the second time? (Everyone had the same base to compare.)

j. Can anyone tell me the mathematical term we use to describe numbers that are based on hundredths? (Percents.) So percent is based on 100. If we look at your fractions, we have everything set up per 100. Does anyone recall how to convert our fractions to an actual percent? (Drop off the denominator, as long as it is 100, and add the percent symbol behind the numerator. Display Visual 6.1. Below each fraction, record the equivalent in 100ths and below that, the percent representation. For example, 1/10 = 10/100 = 10%.)

k. So why would it be useful to have skill in comparing the magnitude of fractions or any other number for that matter? Today we are going to investigate a problem I guarantee you will some day face that requires you to compare numbers. How well you understand the differences in these numbers can and will have an effect on the quality of your life.

l. Whoa, that sounds like a pretty big statement on my part. But every day, people make decisions without fully understanding how important the number differences are, especially in the pocketbook.

m. What I would like you to do right now is put the desks back in rows for me and then find your original group of three. Then seat yourselves so that you can see the front of the room.

n. Today we are going to help Josette, a fifteen-year-old BMX racer make a decision about purchasing a new bike. Now Josette is a champion racer and loves her sport. She would however, very much like to purchase a new bike. What do you suppose would be the major issue for Josette? (Allow the students to speculate and record their responses on the board. Money, time, the type of bike, the availability, etc.)

o. Yes, the big issue is money. Josette must determine how much she really wants the bike and what she is willing to give up to gain the new bike. You and your partners have the job of helping Josette determine what she should do about the bike situation. You will read about Josette's situation in the handout, and as a group, make a decision. You have approximately ten minutes to complete steps 1-6 on the handout.

    p. Distribute Activity 6.1 and allow time for each group to read the scenario and to complete steps 1-6. Allow approximately ten minutes for this activity. Call the groups back to attention and discuss the following:

    q. Who can summarize Josette's problem? (She would like to purchase a new bike, but she has to decide whether to wait for the new bike and pay cash or purchase the bike on credit and pay it off over time.)

    r. Josette must determine whether the benefits of having the bike right now outweigh the extra costs of paying the interest on the loan. Let's make sure we define the words benefits and costs. (Write the words Benefits and Costs on the board and define Benefits as the satisfaction we expect to gain and Costs as what we have to give up.)

4. Discuss the remainder of Activity 6.1 (For answers see Visual 6.2).

5. Distribute Activity 6.2 for homework to be due the following day. (For answers see Visual 6.3.)

Extensions

1. Have the students interview their parents or other family members about their experiences with taking on debt.
2. Ask the students to collect advertisements for credit purchases found in newspapers.

ACTIVITY 6.1 ▲ Josette's Choices

Read about Josette's situation below and answer questions 1-6.

Josette is a 15-year-old who has been racing BMX bicycles for nine years. Josette has been the champion of her age group for the past two years. She is now in the 15-16 year-old group, and she is worried about being able to compete successfully. Josette is thinking about buying a new bike for the upcoming year of competition. The problem is that Josette has only $200 and the bike she would like to purchase sells for $850. Josette earns $65 per week working for her neighbor and she also receives an allowance of $25 per week from her family. Josette's current bike is in pretty good shape. Josette believes that the new bike would make her more competitive this year, but she is worried about the expense of purchasing a new bike. Josette figures that she can put all her work money toward the new bike, plus $5 from her weekly allowance.

Josette has a couple of options to consider. Option 1: She could keep saving her money and when she has earned the full $850, she could buy the bike with cash. Option 2: She could borrow money from her parents, purchase the bike right now, and pay them back over time. Option 3: She could borrow the money from the BMX Association, purchase the bike right now, and pay the association back over time. Option 4: She could purchase the bike on credit from the retailer and pay it back over time. What would you do? Consider the details of each option below and answer the questions that follow. Be prepared to discuss your decision.

Option 1: Pay Cash

Option 2: Borrow the money from her parents at 1/10 of the borrowed amount; pay it back in full within six months

Option 3: Borrow the money from the BMX Association at 6/25 of the borrowed amount; pay it back in full within twelve months.

Option 4: Purchase the bike on credit from the retailer at 8/25 of the borrowed amount; pay it back in full within four months. The dealer has a special deal: if you win a race within six months of purchasing the bike, the bike is free.

1. Use your skill in comparing fractions to convert each fraction in Options 2, 3, and 4 to percents.

   1/10 equals _____%   6/25 equals _____%   8/25 equals _____%

ACTIVITY 6.1 (continued)

2. The way this works is when Josette borrows money to make a purchase she must pay for the use of someone else's money. This charge is called INTEREST on the amount borrowed. Interest is always reported as a percentage of the amount borrowed, and it is calculated on the basis of borrowing the money for one year. This type of interest is easy to calculate and is called SIMPLE INTEREST. Here is how to calculate the interest.

Interest =   Amount Borrowed called Principal   X   Rate   X   Time
I   =   P   X   r   X   t

I is the amount of interest, P is the amount borrowed, r is the percentage rate of interest, t is the time in years.

Calculate the interest payment on each of the options below, using the formula of I=P times r times t.

Option 1:   P = $650, r = 0%, t = 0
Interest = ($650) (0) (0) = _____

Option 2:   P = $650, r = 10%, t = 1/2 year
Interest = ($650) (.10) (1/2) = _____

Option 3:   P = _____, r = _____, t = _____
Interest =

Option 4   P = _____, r = _____, t = _____
Interest =

3. Calculate how long it will take Josette to pay off the money she owes and the interest for each option below:

Option 1 (How many weeks will it take her to save for the new bike?) _____ Weeks

Option 2: (How many weeks will it take to pay off the loan and the interest?) _____ Weeks

Option 3: (How many weeks will it take to pay off the loan and the interest?) _____ Weeks

Option 4: (How many weeks will it take to pay off the loan and the interest?) _____ Weeks

ACTIVITY 6.1 (continued)

4. To help Josette make the decision on which option to choose, let's consider the good points of each option (we will call those BENEFITS) and the downside of each option (the COSTS). Record two Benefits and two Costs for each option.

Option #1 Save for the Bike	Option #2 Borrow from Parents	Option #3 Borrow from the Association	Option #4 Borrow from the Dealer
Benefit #1	Benefit #1	Benefit #1	Benefit #1
Benefit #2	Benefit #2	Benefit #2	Benefit #2
Cost #1	Cost #1	Cost #1	Cost #1
Cost #2	Cost #2	Cost #2	Cost #2

5. Based on the costs and benefits of each option, which option should Josette choose and why?

6. Are there any other options you can think of for Josette to consider in this situation?

ACTIVITY 6.2 ▲ Converting Fractions

1. Convert the following fractions to percents and rank them in order from smallest to largest.

   5/16=

   20/25 =

   3/7 =

   5/14 =

   1/2 =

   100/112 =

   625/400 =

   17/40 =

   50/50 =

   11/77 =

2. Explain how percentages make it easy to compare fractions of unequal size:

   _____

   _____

   _____

3. Make up your own story about a person who must make a decision about whether to pay cash or borrow money to purchase a product. Your story must have the following components:

   Type of product, interest rates, amount to be borrowed, time to pay back the loan, and three options.

VISUAL 6.1

1/10	3/20	1/4	2/5	9/20	3/5	13/20	3/4	4/5	7/8

VISUAL 6.2 ▲ Answers to Activity 6.1

1. Use your skill in comparing fractions to convert each fraction in Options 2, 3, and 4 to percents.

   1/10 equals 10%   6/25 equals 24%   8/25 equals 32%

2. The way this works is when Josette borrows money to make a purchase she must pay for the use of someone else's money. This charge is called INTEREST on the amount borrowed. Interest is always reported as a percentage of the amount borrowed, and it is calculated on the basis of borrowing the money for one year. This type of interest is easy to calculate and is called SIMPLE INTEREST. Here is how to calculate the interest.

Interest	=	Amount Borrowed called Principal	X	Rate	X	Time
I	=	P	X	r	X	t

   I is the amount of interest, P is the amount borrowed, r is the percentage rate of interest, t is the time in years.

   Calculate the interest payment on each of the options below, using the formula of I=P times r times t.

   Option 1:   P = $650, r = 0%, t = 0
   Interest = ($650) (0) (0) = $0

   Option 2:   P = $650, r = 10%, t = 1/2 year
   Interest = ($650) (.10) (1/2) = $32.50

   Option 3:   P = $650, r = 24%, t = 1 year
   Interest = ($650) (.24) (1) = $156.00

   Option 4   P = $650, r = 32%, t = 1/3 year
   Interest = ($650) (.32) (.33) = $68.64

3. Calculate how long it will take Josette to pay off the money she owes and the interest for each option below:

   Option 1 (How many weeks will it take her to save for the new bike?) 10 Weeks

   Option 2: (How many weeks will it take to pay off the loan and the interest?) 10 Weeks

   Option 3: (How many weeks will it take to pay off the loan and the interest?) 12 Weeks

   Option 4: (How many weeks will it take to pay off the loan and the interest?) 11 Weeks

VISUAL 6.2 (continued)

4. To help Josette make the decision on which option to choose, let's consider the good points of each option (we will call those BENEFITS) and the downside of each option (the COSTS). Record two Benefits and two Costs for each option.

Answers will vary and may include the following:

Option #1 Save for the Bike	Option #2 Borrow from Parents	Option #3 Borrow from the Association	Option #4 Borrow from the Dealer
Benefit #1 No interest	Benefit #1 Get the bike right now	Benefit #1 Get the bike right now	Benefit #1 Get the bike right now
Benefit #2 No debt obligation	Benefit #2 Low interest	Benefit #2 Can practice racing on new bike	Benefit #2 Bike may be free
Cost #1 Use old bike	Cost #1 Interest is $32.5	Cost #1 Interest is high at $156	Cost #1 Interest is really high at $208
Cost #2 Wait two months for bike	Cost #2 Money is tied up for 2-6 months	Cost #2 Money is tied up for 3-12 months	Cost #2 Money is tied up for $2\frac{1}{2}$-4 months

5. Based on the costs and benefits of each option, which option should Josette choose and why?

Answers will vary.

6. Are there any other options you can think of for Josette to consider in this situation?

Answers will vary. Students must justify their answers with the comparisons between costs and benefits.

VISUAL 6.3 ▲ Answers to Activity 6.2

1. Convert the following fractions to percents and rank them in order from smallest to largest.

5/16	**equals**	31.25
20/25	**equals**	80.00
3/7	**equals**	42.86
5/14	**equals**	35.71
1/2	**equals**	50.00
100/112	**equals**	89.29
625/400	**equals**	156.25
17/40	**equals**	42.50
50/50	**equals**	100.00
11/77	**equals**	14.29

2. Explain how percentages make it easy to compare fractions of unequal size:

   Percents convert fractions to a common base of 100 and make comparisons possible.

3. Make up your own story about a person who must make a decision about whether to pay cash or borrow money to purchase a product. Your story must have the following components:

   Type of product, interest rates, amount to be borrowed, time to pay back the loan, and three options.

   Scenarios will vary but must include a product, the amount to be borrowed, the rate of interest, the time to pay back the loan, and three possible options.

Fraction Cards—Front

A	B
Fraction Card 3/30	Fraction Card 100/1000
C Fraction Card 80/800	**A** Fraction Card 16/40
B Fraction Card 30/75	**C** Fraction Card 24/60
A Fraction Card 21/28	**B** Fraction Card 36/48
C Fraction Card 63/84	**A** Fraction Card 49/56

B	C
Fraction Card 84/96	Fraction Card 140/160
A Fraction Card 25/100	**B** Fraction Card 13/52
C Fraction Card 36/144	**A** Fraction Card 93/155
B Fraction Card 45/75	**C** Fraction Card 24/40
A Fraction Card 48/60	**B** Fraction Card 92/115

C	A
Fraction Card 68/85	Fraction Card 18/120
B	C
Fraction Card 45/300	Fraction Card 150/1000
A	B
Fraction Card 81/180	Fraction Card 27/60
C	A
Fraction Card 99/220	Fraction Card 65/100
B	C
Fraction Card 156/240	Fraction Card 39/60

Fraction Cards—Back

Step #1– Find your group. There are three people to a group. The groups are based on the fraction written on the other side of this card. Step #2– Once you have located the other two people in your group, find a place to sit and discuss what your group has in common.	Step #1– Find your group. There are three people to a group. The groups are based on the fraction written on the other side of this card. Step #2– Once you have located the other two people in your group, find a place to sit and discuss what your group has in common.
Step #1– Find your group. There are three people to a group. The groups are based on the fraction written on the other side of this card. Step #2– Once you have located the other two people in your group, find a place to sit and discuss what your group has in common.	Step #1– Find your group. There are three people to a group. The groups are based on the fraction written on the other side of this card. Step #2– Once you have located the other two people in your group, find a place to sit and discuss what your group has in common.
Step #1– Find your group. There are three people to a group. The groups are based on the fraction written on the other side of this card. Step #2– Once you have located the other two people in your group, find a place to sit and discuss what your group has in common.	Step #1– Find your group. There are three people to a group. The groups are based on the fraction written on the other side of this card. Step #2– Once you have located the other two people in your group, find a place to sit and discuss what your group has in common.
Step #1– Find your group. There are three people to a group. The groups are based on the fraction written on the other side of this card. Step #2– Once you have located the other two people in your group, find a place to sit and discuss what your group has in common.	Step #1– Find your group. There are three people to a group. The groups are based on the fraction written on the other side of this card. Step #2– Once you have located the other two people in your group, find a place to sit and discuss what your group has in common.
Step #1– Find your group. There are three people to a group. The groups are based on the fraction written on the other side of this card. Step #2– Once you have located the other two people in your group, find a place to sit and discuss what your group has in common.	Step #1– Find your group. There are three people to a group. The groups are based on the fraction written on the other side of this card. Step #2– Once you have located the other two people in your group, find a place to sit and discuss what your group has in common.

Lesson 7

Which Pet is Right For You?

Mathematics Prerequisites

Prior to this lesson, students should know:
- Whole number operations.
- Percents.
- Graphing.

Economics Prerequisites

Prior to this lesson, students should know:
- Benefits.
- Costs.
- Opportunity cost.

Lesson Objectives

Students will be able to:
- Identify factors to consider when purchasing a pet.
- Assign numerical weights as an indicator of relative importance.
- Rank and compare the costs and benefits of various alternatives.
- Present to the class the rationale behind the selection of a particular pet.

Abstract

This lesson focuses on a topic that is at the heart of economics, that of decision making. Decision making from an economic perspective requires individuals to consider both the benefits and costs for each alternative. Human nature, however, often makes this benefit-cost analysis a foregone conclusion as people emphasize the benefits of what they think they want and ignore or minimize the costs of what they think is the less attractive alternative. The students will apply several important mathematics skills in the process of learning about economic decision making. Activity 7.1 calls for the students, working in pairs, to develop selection factors and a weighting scheme to select a particular type of pet. In Activity 7.2, the students work through the process of ranking the desirability of owning a goldfish. The lesson concludes with the students ranking and graphing six pet alternatives and making a pet selection decision. Student teams then present their decisions to the class.

Mathematics Terms

- Whole numbers
- Ranking

➤ Percentage
➤ Weighting

Materials

➤ One copy of Activities 7.1, 7.2 and 7.3 for each student
➤ Transparencies of Activities 7.1, 7.2 and 7.3

Estimated Time

One class period

Warm-Up Activities

Twenty students were surveyed about their school lunch favorites. The results are below:

Favorite Lunch	No. of Students
Hamburgers	5
Tacos	3
Pizza	8
Hot Dogs	4

Write these results as ratios, change them to their percent form, and put them in order with the most favorite first.

Lunch Favorites	Ratio	Percent
Pizza	8/20	40%
Hamburgers	5/20	25%
Hot Dogs	4/20	20%
Tacos	3/20	15%

If you were to put these foods on a ranking scale of –5 to +5 with –5 meaning please don't serve this, and +5 meaning the favorite, how would you rank them? (Answers will vary.) Explain why. (Answers will vary.) Can you think of a couple of foods that you would rank –5? (Answers will vary.) Why? (Answers will vary.)

Procedures

1. Begin the following discussion:
   a. How many of you own a pet? (Acknowledge those students.)
   b. Let's make a list of possible pets for someone to own. (Record student responses on the board.)

    c. Which pet looks like it would be the most fun to own? (Circle two or three of the student choices for a fun pet.)

    d. Is fun the best way to decide on a type of pet? (Consider student responses.)

    e. What are some other factors that might be important in selecting a pet? (Record student responses. You may need to guide the discussion toward factors such as size, how much it eats, high or low maintenance, veterinary bills, food, space, companionship, protection, housing.)

    f. Thank you for that fine discussion on the factors that one should consider when selecting a pet. You will now have an opportunity to design your own scheme for pet selection. We will begin with having you pair up, complete several activities, and then present to the class your solution to the problem of selecting a pet.

2. Divide the students into teams of two in any manner you choose. Distribute Activity 7.1. Review the directions with students.

3. Allow approximately five minutes for the students to complete Part 1 of Activity 7.1.

4. Call the groups back to attention. Discuss Part 1 with the entire class. Ask each team to write one of its factors on the board.

5. Once all the factors are up on the board, announce to the group that it might be helpful to classify the factors into two separate groups. Write the words "Cost" and "Time" on the board.

6. Tell the students that the Cost grouping represents any dollar expense associated with owning a pet. (Factors that fit into this group might include the purchase price, food, grooming, veterinary visits, etc.)

7. Tell the students that the Time grouping represents any type of effort associated with a particular type of pet. (Factors that fit into this group might include exercising, attention, feeding, care, etc.)

8. Begin classifying each factor listed on the board into one or both of the groups by writing the factor under its appropriate heading. It is possible that the groups may not be mutually exclusive. Once all factors have been grouped, distribute Activity 7.2. Instruct the students to complete Part 2 of Activity 7.1. Allow approximately 10 minutes for completion of Part 2.

9. Call the groups back to attention. Display the transparency of Activity 7.2. Discuss Part 2 of Activity 7.1, making sure the students have correctly weighted, ranked, and totaled scores for the goldfish.

10. Display the transparency of Activity 7.3, *Pet Selection Chart*. Ask for a Cost and Time score from a student team and plot the point. Label

the point "Goldfish." Review with the students the significance of each quadrant.

11. Distribute Activity 7.3, *Pet Selection Chart*. Instruct the students to complete Part 3 of Activity 7.1. Review the instructions for calculating Cost and Time scores. Allow approximately 15 minutes for completion of Part 3.

12. Call the groups back to attention. Ask if anyone would like to volunteer to share her/his pet selection decision. Allow several students to discuss their choice and the reasons behind the choice. State the following:

    a. Selecting a pet can be a complicated decision, especially when your time and money are involved. Whenever you have an important decision to make it is important to list the factors, give them a weight of importance, and then rank your alternatives.

    b. In today's activity, we had several alternatives for a pet, from rats to cats to horses. How did we decide which pet was best? (Developed selection factors, weighted the factors, and ranked each alternative.)

    c. How did our mathematics skills assist us in making the best decision? (Assigning weights, computing totals, plotting points.)

    d. Are there any wrong pet selections in today's activity? (No.) As long as a person fairly and honestly assigns weights and rankings there cannot be an incorrect selection. We all have different opinions on what we value and what we don't value. This decision process simply helps us understand more fully what our values are and their level of importance.

13. As homework, assign the students the task of applying the decision-making process to another decision. This decision must have three alternatives and at least four selection factors. Ask the students to be prepared to present their scenario, complete with factors, alternatives, weights, and scores.

ACTIVITY 7.1

Part 1

You and your partner are charged with the task of setting up a system for selecting a pet. Your system will include some important features that will assist you in selecting the right pet. The first things to consider in the selection process are the factors you and your partner think are important to consider when looking for a pet. In the space below, brainstorm 15 factors that might be important in selecting a pet. If you and your partner are having difficulty coming up with factors, think about why most people don't have elephants as pets and why many people own goldfish.

ACTIVITY 7.1 (continued)

Part 2

Follow steps A-H to complete the chart on Activity 7.2.

A.   Select four factors from your list in Part 1 or the list on the board that you and your partner think are most important in the area of Cost; record these factors in the space provided in Activity 7.2.

B.   Select four factors from your list in Part 1 or the list on the board that you and your partner think are most important in the area of Time; record these factors in the space provided in Activity 7.2.

C & D.   You and your partner will now determine the weight to give each factor. The weights will be based on 100 percent. The weights you assign the four factors must total to 100. As an example if each factor had equal importance, their weights would each be 25. Assign weights for each factor in Columns C and D.

Time-out everyone. Let's review for a moment to make sure it's clear what is going on here. In the space provided, briefly summarize what the factors represent:

Factors are:_____

_____

In the space provided, briefly summarize why the weights must sum to 100:

Weights show:_____

_____

E & F.   Now you are ready to determine whether or not a certain type of pet is the best for you and your group. Let's consider a goldfish. Is that the best pet for you? You can find out if you are well suited to owning a goldfish by completing the table. On each factor, you will rate the goldfish on a scale from –5 to +5. –5 represents no effort or Cost and 5 represents very high effort or Cost. For example, if you looked at a factor like exercise, a goldfish would rate a -5 because you don't have to expend any effort; the goldfish has it all under control. Rank the goldfish on each of the factors in the Cost group and the Time group.

G.   Once you have the ranking for each of the four Cost factors, you are ready to calculate a total for each factor. Simply multiply the value in Column C times the value in Column E and record the result in Column G. Complete this process for each factor in the Cost group. Add the totals in Column G and record this as the Cost Score.

H.   Once you have the ranking for each of the four Time factors, you are ready to calculate a total score for each factor. Simply multiply the value in Column D times the value in Column F and record the result in Column H. Complete this process for each factor in the Time group. Add the totals in Column H and record this as the Time Score.

ACTIVITY 7.1 (continued)

Part 3

1. Plot and label the Goldfish Scores on the Pet Selection Chart on Activity 7.3.

2. Using your weight scheme from Activity 7.2, calculate the Cost and Time scores for the following six pets and record in the space provided.

Pet	Cost Score	Time Score
Large dog		
Snake		
Cat		
Horse		
Rat		
Tarantella		

3. Plot and label the pets on the Pet Selection Chart.

4. How would you characterize the type of pet that occupies Quadrant IV? Quadrant I?

5. How would you have to modify the Pet Selection Chart on Activity 7.3 to add a third category of factors?

6. So, which pet is best for you? You and your partner will decide which pet is best for you, and why, and you must be prepared to share the reasons for your decision.

ACTIVITY 7.2

COST

A. Group Factors	C. Weight (0-100)	E. Rank (-5 to +5)	G. Total
1.			
2.			
3.			
4.			

COST Score = _____

TIME

B. Group Factors	D. Weight (0-100)	F. Rank (-5 to +5)	H. Total
1.			
2.			
3.			
4.			

Time Score = _____

Goldfish Cost Score = _____   Goldfish Time Score = _____

ACTIVITY 7.3 ▲ Pet Selection Chart

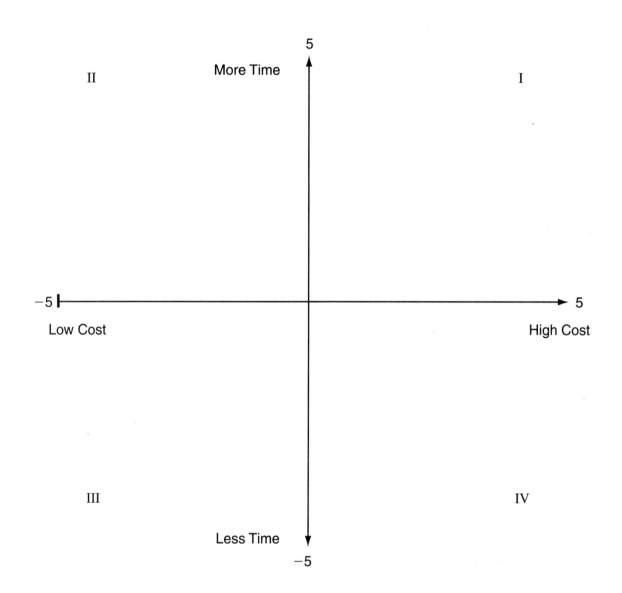

Could You Earn a Million Dollars?

Mathematics Prerequisites

Prior to this lesson, students should know:
- Multiplication.
- Mean.
- Median.
- Range.
- Scatter plots.

Lesson Objectives

Students will be able to:
- Define *earnings* and *human capital*.
- Calculate annual earnings based on an hourly rate.
- Organize and analyze data on education and earnings.
- Make conjectures about the correlation between educational attainment and earnings.
- Calculate the difference in lifetime earnings for people with differing levels of education.

Abstract

This lesson is designed to acquaint students with the relationship between earnings and education. The data are very clear regarding one's earning potential and educational attainment. That is, the more education an individual has the greater his or her earning potential. This is an important lesson for the students to explore as they begin forming opinions about the value of school and their own education. The students will use their mathematics skills to explore the relationship between earnings and education. They will also define earnings and human capital.

Mathematics Terms

- Whole Number Operations
- Mean, Median, and Range
- Process-algorithms for use in calculating yearly earnings from an hourly wage
- Graphical representations for a data set

Materials

- One copy of Activities 8.1 and 8.2 for each student
- Transparencies of Visuals 8.1 - 8.3

> ➤ Education Playing Cards (one card for half the class)
> ➤ Earnings Playing Cards (one card for half the class)

Estimated Time

One class period

Warm-Up Activities

Your company is testing portable CD players. The machines (denoted by letters A-T, below) are run for a number of hours equivalent to the number of months of normal use. Here is the number of months the tested machines would last:

Group 1

Machine	months	Machine	months	Machine	months	Machine	months
A	127	F	145	K	153	P	139
B	181	G	186	L	160	Q	52
C	36	H	182	M	122	R	152
D	142	I	148	N	150	S	136
E	116	J	188	O	163	T	202

A new set of tests was run with new, more expensive gear. Here are the new test results:

Group 2

Machine	months	Machine	months	Machine	months	Machine	months
A	142	F	135	K	162	P	149
B	128	G	144	L	122	Q	152
C	180	H	218	M	142	R	130
D	146	I	123	N	138	S	140
E	144	J	156	O	139	T	150

Find the mean, median and range for each set of data.

Group 1	
Mean	144
Median	149
Range	166

Group 2	
Mean	147
Median	143
Range	96

Should the company switch to the new gear? Write a paragraph explaining why or why not.

Procedures

1. Display Visual 8.1 as the students are entering the classroom.

2. Discuss the following:
   a. Do you think you could earn a million dollars? (Allow the students to speculate.)
   b. Who can define the word "earn"? (Record student responses on the board.) Let's summarize these suggestions by saying that earnings are what a person gains when he or she performs work. (Write this definition on the board. An example might be "A person earns $25 for mowing a lawn.")
   c. What type of work do you think it would it take to earn a million dollars? (Allow the students to brainstorm their ideas and record them on the board. Answers may include professional athletes, doctors, scientists, winning the lottery.)
   d. Today we will discover a foolproof method for earning a million dollars.

   Direct each student to bring his or her calculator, a pencil and a sheet of paper to the front of the room. Push all the desks back from the center of the room, leaving yourself a clear path to the board **(see room layout at the end of the lesson)**. With a roll of masking tape, lay down a line that splits the room in half.

4. Divide the students evenly into the two zones and ask them to sit down on the floor.

5. On the board, draw a line to divide the space in half. Write the word "EDUCATION" on the left side and the word "EARNINGS" on the right side. Explain that the room is divided in the same way, with the students in the left zone representing education and the students in the right zone representing earnings.

6. Ask for a definition of education from the students in the education zone and record responses on the board under the word "EDUCA-TION." (Learning, years in school, college.)

7. Ask for a definition of earnings from the students in the earnings zone and record responses on the board under the word "EARNINGS." (The amount of money received in a period of time in exchange for working.)

8. Announce that the students will receive a playing card representing his or her zone. Distribute an education playing card to each student in the education zone and an earnings playing card to each student in the earnings zone. Ask the students to read their cards quietly.

9. Announce that each card has a match in the other zone. Direct the students to find their partners in the other zone and to sit down together in either zone.

10. Once everyone has a settled, ask each pair to calculate the yearly earnings for the person on their card.

11. Allow a few minutes for this activity; then ask if anyone has an easy procedure for turning hourly earnings into earnings for a whole year. (Write student procedure on the board. Examples: For eight hours in a working day, 5 days in a week, 52 weeks in a year, the procedure would be to multiply [(hourly earnings)*(8)*(5)*(52)].)

12. Determine a standard procedure. (Do people actually work every day of the year and should we consider giving our people two weeks of vacation?) How many weeks should we multiply by? (50) Ask each group to use the same procedure.

13. Take another piece of masking tape and divide the room into fourths (see the room layout suggestions at the end of the lesson). Using additional pieces of tape, label the four zones, I, II, III, IV. Instruct each pair of students to occupy one of the four zones based on their level of education. Zone I, not a HS graduate; Zone II, HS graduate; Zone III, some college; Zone IV, college graduate.

14. Within each zone, ask the students to use their math skills to summarize the earnings data for everyone in their zone by following the instructions on the back of their earnings playing card. (Students are directed to formulate the range, median, and mode for the yearly earnings levels represented in their group.)

15. On the board, create four columns labeled Zone I, Zone II, Zone III, and Zone IV. Ask a representative from each zone to record his or her summary data in the appropriate column.

16. Ask each pair of students to predict what the data on the board represents and to write this prediction on a piece of paper.

17. Ask the students to help you reassemble the room and sit with their partners. Distribute Activity 8.1 and instruct each pair of students to follow the directions in completing a scatter plot of the education-earnings data.

18. Once the students have finished with their scatter plots, display Visual 8.2 and discuss Activity 8.1. (Visual 8.2 shows answers to "Yearly Earnings" in Activity 8.1.)

19. Discuss the following:
    a. Who had a person in Zone I? (Select a pair of students.) How much education did your person have? (Not a high school graduate.)

What do you think would be the best way for your person to move into Zone II? (Get a High School diploma; if the response is "earn more money," be sure to ask how the person could earn more money.)

b. What about moving from Zone II to Zone III? Why would a person want to move from Zone II to Zone III? How do you move from Zone II to Zone III? (Make more money; improve your lifestyle, etc. Get more education.)

c. Yes, more education is a key to moving from a lower Zone to a higher Zone; it is the key to earning higher income. In other words you've got to "Learn to Earn." (Write "Learn to Earn" on the board.) People who move from a lower zone to a higher zone, getting more education and learning new skills, are actually improving something we call human capital. (Write "Human Capital" on the board.)

d. Has anyone heard of the word "capital" before? (Responses may include things like capital cities.) Your capital, your human capital, the skills you bring to the workplace. (Write this definition under "Human Capital")

e. Improving your human capital is a key to moving from a lower zone to a higher zone; it is the key to improving your earnings. When you learn a new skill, you have the potential to gain higher earnings.

f. At the beginning of the period, I asked if you could earn a million dollars. Well, given the earnings we have investigated today, which zones include people capable of earning a million dollars over their working lifetimes? (Allow speculation.)

g. Let's see if you can calculate a lifetime of earnings for the person on your card. How many years do you think people work in their lifetimes? (Allow speculation.) Suppose we say that the average person has 40 years to work. Could you calculate how much your person would earn, in total, in those 40 years? (Multiply the yearly earnings by 40.)

h. Okay, which cards will earn a million dollars over 40 years? (Zone III people are close and everyone in Zone IV.)

i. Do you have to be rich and famous to earn a million dollars? (No, just go to college.)

Closure

1. State the following:
   a. People use their human capital to earn a living, and the ability to earn is based on education. You must learn to earn, and the key to earning a good living is to improve your human capital.

   b. On a piece of paper, I want you to explain how you would move your playing card person to the next zone using our new vocabulary words *earnings* and *human capital*. (Allow several minutes for students to write their statements.)

   c. Who will share their summary statement? (An example might be, Skyler could improve his human capital by getting his GED. With a GED, Skyler could find a better-paying job and increase his earnings.)

   d. Distribute Activity 8.2 for homework. (Answers are given on Visual 8.3.)

ACTIVITY 8.1 ▲ Yearly Earnings

1. Complete the table by calculating the earnings for each person.

Name	Zone	Hourly Earnings	Yearly Earnings	Name	Zone	Hourly Earnings	Yearly Earnings
Hannah	I	$ 5.50		Sara	III	$10.75	
Shingo	I	$ 5.75		Manuel	III	$10.75	
Skyler	I	$ 6.00		Kaydee	III	$11.00	
Jared	I	$ 6.25		Ian	III	$11.25	
Kayla	I	$ 6.50		Sherice	III	$11.50	
Kyle	I	$ 7.00		Devon	III	$11.75	
Kali	I	$ 7.25		Tabetha	III	$12.00	
Dylan	I	$ 7.50		Levi	III	$12.25	
Sabrina	II	$ 8.50		Jaselle	IV	$15.00	
Demitri	II	$ 8.75		Newt	IV	$15.25	
Mackenzie	II	$ 9.00		Felicia	IV	$16.00	
Miguel	II	$ 9.25		Cesar	IV	$16.25	
Tatiana	II	$ 9.50		Banessa	IV	$16.50	
Chan	II	$10.00		Zach	IV	$17.00	
Kira	II	$10.25		Mikaela	IV	$17.25	
Juan	II	$10.50		Ivan	IV	$17.50	

2. Use the space below to create a graphical representation of earnings and education zones.

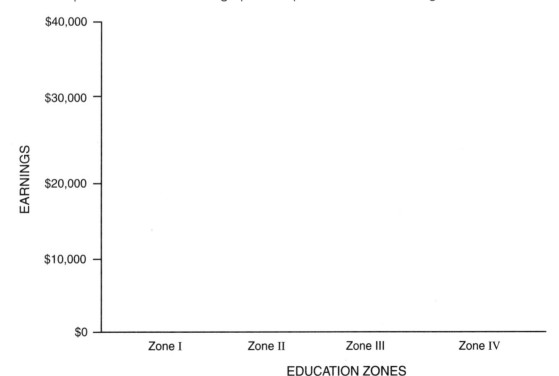

ACTIVITY 8.2 ▲ Lifetime Earnings

Name	Zone	Hourly Earnings	Yearly Earnings	40 Years of Earnings	Name	Zone	Hourly Earnings	Yearly Earnings	40 Years of Earnings
Hannah	I	$ 5.50	$11,000		Sara	III	$10.75	$21,500	
Shingo	I	$ 5.75	$11,500		Manuel	III	$10.75	$21,500	
Skyler	I	$ 6.00	$12,000		Kaydee	III	$11.00	$22,000	
Jared	I	$ 6.25	$12,500		Ian	III	$11.25	$22,500	
Kayla	I	$ 6.50	$13,000		Sherice	III	$11.50	$23,000	
Kyle	I	$ 7.00	$14,000		Devon	III	$11.75	$23,500	
Kali	I	$ 7.25	$14,500		Tabetha	III	$12.00	$24,000	
Dylan	I	$ 7.50	$15,000		Levi	III	$12.25	$24,500	
Sabrina	II	$ 8.50	$17,000		Jaselle	IV	$15.00	$30,000	
Demitri	II	$ 8.75	$17,500		Newt	IV	$15.25	$30,500	
Mackenzie	II	$ 9.00	$18,000		Felicia	IV	$16.00	$32,000	
Miguel	II	$ 9.25	$18,500		Cesar	IV	$16.25	$32,500	
Tatiana	II	$ 9.50	$19,000		Banessa	IV	$16.50	$33,000	
Chan	II	$10.00	$20,000		Zach	IV	$17.00	$34,000	
Kira	II	$10.25	$20,500		Mikaela	IV	$17.25	$34,500	
Juan	II	$10.50	$21,000		Ivan	IV	$17.50	$35,000	

1. Calculate the lifetime of earnings and record the amount in the 40-Year column.

2. Calculate the mean lifetime of earnings for each zone and record the amounts below:

   Zone I _____

   Zone II _____

   Zone III _____

   Zone IV _____

3. What is the difference in mean earnings, over 40 years, from Zone I to Zone II? $_____

4. What is the difference in mean earnings, over 40 years, from Zone II to Zone III? $_____

5. What is the difference in mean earnings, over 40 years, from Zone III to Zone IV? $_____

6. What is the difference in mean earnings, over 40 years, from Zone I to Zone IV? $_____

7. What is the value of graduating from high school? $_____

COULD YOU EARN

A MILLION

DOLLARS?

1. Complete the table by calculating the earnings for each person:

Name	Earnings	Income	Name	Earnings	Income
Hannah	$ 5.50	$11,000	Sara	$10.75	$21,500
Shingo	$ 5.75	$11,500	Manuel	$10.75	$21,500
Skyler	$ 6.00	$12,000	Kaydee	$11.00	$22,000
Jared	$ 6.25	$12,500	Ian	$11.25	$22,500
Kayla	$ 6.50	$13,000	Sherice	$11.50	$23,000
Kyle	$ 7.00	$14,000	Devon	$11.75	$23,500
Kali	$ 7.25	$14,500	Tabetha	$12.00	$24,000
Dylan	$ 7.50	$15,000	Levi	$12.25	$24,500
Sabrina	$ 8.50	$17,000	Jaselle	$15.00	$30,000
Demitri	$ 8.75	$17,500	Newt	$15.25	$30,500
Mackenzie	$ 9.00	$18,000	Felicia	$16.00	$32,000
Miguel	$ 9.25	$18,500	Cesar	$16.25	$32,500
Tatiana	$ 9.50	$19,000	Banessa	$16.50	$33,000
Chan	$10.00	$20,000	Zach	$17.00	$34,000
Kira	$10.25	$20,500	Mikaela	$17.25	$34,500
Juan	$10.50	$21,000	Ivan	$17.50	$35,000

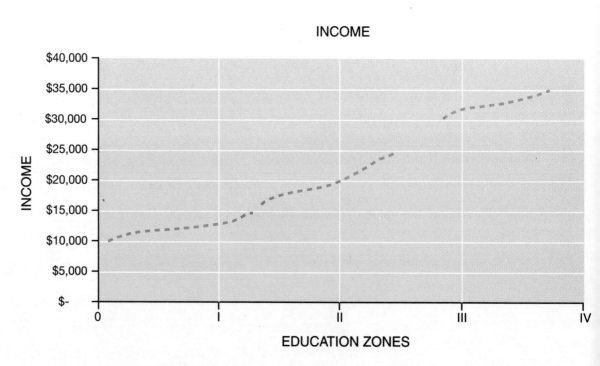

INCOME

EDUCATION ZONES

2. Use the space below to create a graphical representation of earnings and education zone:

VISUAL 8.3 ▲ Answers to Activity 8.2

1. Calculate the lifetime of earnings and record the amount in the 40-Year column:

Name	Zone	Income	40 Years	Name	Zone	Earnings	Income	40 Years
Hannah	I	$11,000	$440,000	Sara	III	$10.75	$21,500	$ 860,000
Shingo	I	$11,500	$460,000	Manuel	III	$10.75	$21,500	$ 860,000
Skyler	I	$12,000	$480,000	Kaydee	III	$11.00	$22,000	$ 880,000
Jared	I	$12,500	$500,000	Ian	III	$11.25	$22,500	$ 900,000
Kayla	I	$13,000	$520,000	Sherice	III	$11.50	$23,000	$ 920,000
Kyle	I	$14,000	$560,000	Devon	III	$11.75	$23,500	$ 940,000
Kali	I	$14,500	$580,000	Tabetha	III	$12.00	$24,000	$ 960,000
Dylan	I	$15,000	$600,000	Levi	III	$12.25	$24,500	$ 980,000
Sabrina	II	$17,000	$680,000	Jaselle	IV	$15.00	$30,000	$1,200,000
Demitri	II	$17,500	$700,000	Newt	IV	$15.25	$30,500	$1,220,000
Mackenzie	II	$18,000	$720,000	Felicia	IV	$16.00	$32,000	$1,280,000
Miguel	II	$18,500	$740,000	Cesar	IV	$16.25	$32,500	$1,300,000
Tatiana	II	$19,000	$760,000	Banessa	IV	$16.50	$33,000	$1,320,000
Chan	II	$20,000	$800,000	Zach	IV	$17.00	$34,000	$1,360,000
Kira	II	$20,500	$820,000	Mikaela	IV	$17.25	$34,500	$1,380,000
Juan	II	$21,000	$840,000	Ivan	IV	$17.50	$35,000	$1,400,000

2. Calculate the mean lifetime of earnings for each zone and record the amounts below:
   Zone I: $517,500
   Zone II: $757,500
   Zone III: $912,500
   Zone IV: $1,307,500

3. What is the difference in mean earnings, over 40 years, from Zone I to Zone II? $240,000

4. What is the difference in mean earnings, over 40 years, from Zone II to Zone III? $155,000

5. What is the difference in mean earnings, over 40 years, from Zone III to Zone IV? $395,000

6. What is the difference in mean earnings, over 40 years, from Zone I to Zone IV? $790,000

7. What is the value of graduating from high school? $240,00

Earnings Cards: Front

INCOME

Name - Hannah

Earning $5.5

INCOME

Name - Shingo

Earning $5.75

INCOME

Name - Skyler

Earning $6

INCOME

Name - Jared

Earning $6.25

INCOME

Name - Kayla

Earning $6.5

INCOME

Name - Kyle

Earning $7

INCOME

Name - Kali

Earning $7.25

INCOME

Name - Dylan

Earning $7.5

Earnings Cards: Front (continued)

INCOME	INCOME
Name - Sabrina	Name - Demitri
Earning $8.5	Earning $8.75

INCOME	INCOME
Name - Mackenzie	Name - Miguel
Earning $9	Earning $9.25

INCOME	INCOME
Name - Tatiana	Name - Chan
Earning $9.5	Earning $10

INCOME	INCOME
Name - Kira	Name - Juan
Earning $10.25	Earning $10.5

Earnings Cards: Front (continued)

INCOME

Name - Sara

Earning $10.75

INCOME

Name - Manuel

Earning $10.75

INCOME

Name - Kaydee

Earning $11

INCOME

Name - Ian

Earning $11.25

INCOME

Name - Sherice

Earning $11.5

INCOME

Name - Devon

Earning $11.75

INCOME

Name - Tabetha

Earning $12

INCOME

Name - Levi

Earning $12.25

Earnings Cards: Front (continued)

INCOME Name - Jaselle Earning $15	INCOME Name - Newt Earning $15.25
INCOME Name - Felicia Earning $16	INCOME Name - Cesar Earning $16.25
INCOME Name - Banessa Earning $16.5	INCOME Name - Zach Earning $17
INCOME Name - Mikaela Earning $17.25	INCOME Name - Ivan Earning $17.5

Earnings Cards: Front (continued)

INCOME

Name -

Earning $

INCOME

Name -

Earning $

INCOME

Name -

Earning $

INCOME

Name -

Earning $

INCOME

Name -

Earning $

INCOME

Name -

Earning $

INCOME

Name -

Earning $

INCOME

Name -

Earning $

Earnings Cards: Back

1 2 3 4 5 6 7 8 Zone # _____	1. Record your zone number in the space below. 2. Record the incomes for each person in your zone. 3. Calculate the range, median, and mode for your zone.

1 2 3 4 5 6 7 8 Zone # _____	1. Record your zone number in the space below. 2. Record the incomes for each person in your zone. 3. Calculate the range, median, and mode for your zone.

1 2 3 4 5 6 7 8 Zone # _____	1. Record your zone number in the space below. 2. Record the incomes for each person in your zone. 3. Calculate the range, median, and mode for your zone.

1 2 3 4 5 6 7 8 Zone # _____	1. Record your zone number in the space below. 2. Record the incomes for each person in your zone. 3. Calculate the range, median, and mode for your zone.

1 2 3 4 5 6 7 8 Zone # _____	1. Record your zone number in the space below. 2. Record the incomes for each person in your zone. 3. Calculate the range, median, and mode for your zone.

1 2 3 4 5 6 7 8 Zone # _____	1. Record your zone number in the space below. 2. Record the incomes for each person in your zone. 3. Calculate the range, median, and mode for your zone.

1 2 3 4 5 6 7 8 Zone # _____	1. Record your zone number in the space below. 2. Record the incomes for each person in your zone. 3. Calculate the range, median, and mode for your zone.

1 2 3 4 5 6 7 8 Zone # _____	1. Record your zone number in the space below. 2. Record the incomes for each person in your zone. 3. Calculate the range, median, and mode for your zone.

Earnings Cards: Back

1 2 3 4 5 6 7 8 Zone # _____	1. Record your zone number in the space below. 2. Record the incomes for each person in your zone. 3. Calculate the range, median, and mode for your zone.

1 2 3 4 5 6 7 8 Zone # _____	1. Record your zone number in the space below. 2. Record the incomes for each person in your zone. 3. Calculate the range, median, and mode for your zone.

1 2 3 4 5 6 7 8 Zone # _____	1. Record your zone number in the space below. 2. Record the incomes for each person in your zone. 3. Calculate the range, median, and mode for your zone.

1 2 3 4 5 6 7 8 Zone # _____	1. Record your zone number in the space below. 2. Record the incomes for each person in your zone. 3. Calculate the range, median, and mode for your zone.

1 2 3 4 5 6 7 8 Zone # _____	1. Record your zone number in the space below. 2. Record the incomes for each person in your zone. 3. Calculate the range, median, and mode for your zone.

1 2 3 4 5 6 7 8 Zone # _____	1. Record your zone number in the space below. 2. Record the incomes for each person in your zone. 3. Calculate the range, median, and mode for your zone.

1 2 3 4 5 6 7 8 Zone # _____	1. Record your zone number in the space below. 2. Record the incomes for each person in your zone. 3. Calculate the range, median, and mode for your zone.

1 2 3 4 5 6 7 8 Zone # _____	1. Record your zone number in the space below. 2. Record the incomes for each person in your zone. 3. Calculate the range, median, and mode for your zone.

Education Cards

EDUCATION	EDUCATION
Name - Hannah	Name - Shingo
Level of Education - Not a High School graduate	Level of Education - Not a High School graduate
Details - finished 8th grade	Details - finished 8th grade
EDUCATION	EDUCATION
Name - Skyler	Name - Jared
Level of Education- Not a High School graduate	Level of Education - Not a High School graduate
Details - finished 9th grade	Details - finished 9th grade
EDUCATION	EDUCATION
Name - Kayla	Name - Kyle
Level of Education- Not a High School graduate	Level of Education - Not a High School graduate
Details - finished 10th grade	Details - finished 10th grade
EDUCATION	EDUCATION
Name - Kali	Name - Dylan
Level of Education- Not a High School graduate	Level of Education - Not a High School graduate
Details - finished 11th grade	Details - finished 11th grade

Education Cards (continued)

EDUCATION

Name - Sabrina

Level of Education - High School graduate

Details - Went straight to work after high school

EDUCATION

Name - Demitri

Level of Educatio - High School graduate

Details - Went straight to work after high school

EDUCATION

Name - Mackenzie

Level of Education - High School graduate

Details - Went straight to work after high school

EDUCATION

Name - Miguel

Level of Education - High School graduate

Details - Went straight to work after high school

EDUCATION

Name - Tatiana

Level of Education - High School graduate

Details - Went straight to work after high school

EDUCATION

Name - Chan

Level of Education - High School graduate

Details - Went straight to work after high school

EDUCATION

Name - Kira

Level of Education - High School graduate

Details - Went straight to work after high school

EDUCATION

Name - Juan

Level of Education - High School graduate

Details - Went straight to work after high school

Education Cards (continued)

EDUCATION	EDUCATION
Name - Sara	Name - Manuel
Level of Education - Some college or training	Level of Education - Some college or training
Details - On the job training	Details - On the job training
EDUCATION	EDUCATION
Name - Kaydee	Name - Ian
Level of Education - Some college or training	Level of Education - Some college or training
Details - On the job training	Details - On the job training
EDUCATION	EDUCATION
Name - Sherice	Name - Devon
Level of Education - Some college or training	Level of Education - Some college or training
Details - On the job training	Details - On the job training
EDUCATION	EDUCATION
Name - Tabetha	Name - Levi
Level of Education - Some college or training	Level of Education - Some college or training
Details - On the job training	Details - On the job training

Education Cards (continued)

EDUCATION

Name - Jaselle

Level of Education - college graduate

Details - Completed 4 - year degree

EDUCATION

Name - Newt

Level of Education - college graduate

Details - Completed 4 - year degree

EDUCATION

Name - Felicia

Level of Education - college graduate

Details - Completed 4 - year degree

EDUCATION

Name - Cesar

Level of Education - college graduate

Details - Completed 4 - year degree

EDUCATION

Name - Banessa

Level of Education - college graduate

Details - Completed 4 - year degree

EDUCATION

Name - Zach

Level of Education - college graduate

Details - Completed 4 - year degree

EDUCATION

Name - Mikaela

Level of Education - college graduate

Details - Completed 4 - year degree

EDUCATION

Name - Ivan

Level of Education - college graduate

Details - Completed 4 - year degree

Education Cards (continued)

EDUCATION Name - Level of Education - Details -	EDUCATION Name - Level of Education - Details -
EDUCATION Name - Level of Education - Details -	EDUCATION Name - Level of Education - Details -
EDUCATION Name - Level of Education - Details -	EDUCATION Name - Level of Education - Details -
EDUCATION Name - Level of Education - Details -	EDUCATION Name - Level of Education - Details -

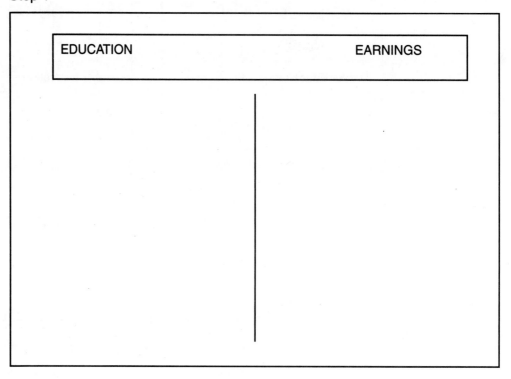

Room Layout Suggestions

Step 1

EDUCATION	EARNINGS

Step 2

EDUCATION	EARNINGS

I II

IV III

Deserted Island

Mathematics Prerequisites

Prior to this lesson, students should know:
- Range.
- Median.
- Box and whisker plots.
- Prediction.
- Whole number operations.

Lesson Objectives

Students will be able to:
- Create and interpret data based on a box and whisker plot (five-point data summary).
- Operate within a specified budget to achieve a desired outcome in a simulated labor market.
- Make predictions regarding the value of labor in the marketplace.

Abstract

This lesson is designed to introduce students to the idea that not all skills are valued equally in the marketplace. The students will explore these differences using their mathematics skills to create box and whisker plots. They will generate their own data on the value of skills by using a bidding activity. The students are given a budget and instructed to purchase the skills needed to survive on a deserted island.

Mathematics Terms

- Basic operations
- Median, range
- Projections

Materials

- One copy of Activities 9.1, 9.2 and 9.3 for each student
- Transparencies of Visuals 9.1 and 9.2
- Occupational Bid Sheets–24 copies
- Masking tape

Estimated Time

One class period

Warm-Up Activities

Tell the students that they are to look up the ages of the 43 Presidents of the United States at the time of their inauguration. The students should do this research themselves; however, you may want to give the data to some students, (as an adaptation for example) so here is the list of ages in order beginning with Washington:

57, 61, 57, 57, 58, 57, 61, 54, 68, 51, 49, 64, 50, 48
65, 52, 56, 46, 54, 49, 51, 47, 55, 55, 54, 42, 51, 56, 55
51, 54, 51, 60, 62, 43, 55, 56, 61, 52, 69, 64, 46, 54

Find the mean, median, upper and lower quartiles. (Mean 54.8, median 55, upper quartile 60.5, and lower quartile 51)

Use these data to see if you can spot any trends or come to any conclusions. For example, could you use the data to predict the ages of future presidents? (Answers will vary.)

An interesting variation of the lesson would be to break the data into thirds (14, 15,and 14), make box plots on the three sets of data, and compare your results for any trends or similarities.

Find the mean, median, upper and lower quartiles for these groups.

Group 1: mean 56.6, median 57, upper quartile 61, lower quartile 50
Group 2: mean 52.5, median 54, upper quartile 55.5, lower quartile 49
Group 3: mean 55.6, median 54.5, upper quartile 61, lower quartile 51

Procedures

1. Display Visual 9.1 as the students are arriving at class. Begin class with the following discussion:
   a. Okay, what kind of skills would you want the people on the island to possess? (Record student responses on the board.)
   b. What criteria or rule of thumb might you use for selecting the people you would want on the island? After all, you will have to survive without the ordinary things we take for granted. (Record student responses on the board. Encourage responses that go beyond people who are "good-looking" or "fun." Encourage consideration of skills that would be beneficial on a deserted island.)
   c. Well, let's take this a bit further and actually look at skills that would be good to have on a deserted island. How would you define the word "skill"? (Write "Skill" on the board and record student responses below. Skill can be defined as an activity that a person is good at doing or has expertise in doing.)
   d. People can earn a living from their skills. When they do, we tend to call that an occupation. (Write "Occupation" on the board next to "Skill.")

e. If you were going to hire someone to help you survive on a deserted island, do you think some skills would be more useful than others? (Yes.)

f. You and a partner will have the chance to select an all-star lineup for your deserted island. Your mission will be to select up to five people to help you and your partner survive on the island. Now remember, the island is completely isolated, uninhabited, and extremely primitive. You will have the opportunity to compete for the team of people you want to bring to the island. We have a limited number of workers available and you and your partner must bid against everyone else in the room for the team of your choice.

2. Group the students into pairs and distribute Activity 9.1. Read the instructions on Activity 9.1 to the class. Assign a Team Letter to each group and have the students record their letter in the space provided on Activity 9.1. Direct the students to select their all-star team and select a bid price for each occupation, staying within the $150,000 budget. (Allow approximately 10 minutes for this activity.)

3. Once each group has completed its selections, direct the groups to fold their bid sheets in half to conceal the bids and pass them up to the front of the room. Mix up the bid sheets and redistribute one bid sheet to each pair of students. The idea is to have each pair of students reporting bid data that is not their own.

4. The students may now look at the bid sheet data (Activity 9.1) they were just given. Using tape, affix 24 Occupational Bid Sheets along the chalk or white board, writing one occupation on each of the Occupational Bid Sheets (this can be done in advance). Ask each pair of students to record the five bids and Team Letter on the appropriate Occupational Bid Sheets.

5. Once everyone has recorded the bid data, direct the students to return to their desks, sitting with their partners. Discuss the following:

a. Let's take a look at the bid data. We will take our top six occupations based on the number of bids. Which occupations have the most bids? (This information will vary, but potential occupations are the Navy Seal, a nurse, or a science teacher.)

b. Why did some occupations have many bids and others have hardly any bids? (Some occupations are more desirable for surviving on a deserted island than other occupations.)

c. Does it look like all occupations are equally valued? (No.)

d. You and your partner will investigate in greater detail the most advantageous occupations for surviving on a deserted island. Your investigation will call for you to create a special graphic that summarizes all this information. This graphic is called a box and whisker plot.

e. We will collect and organize data for the top six occupations and then create a box and whisker plot for each occupation.

6. Distribute Activity 9.2. Gather the top six occupations based on the number of bids. (These are the Occupational Bid Sheets affixed around the classroom. Examples may be the Navy Seal, a nurse, or science teacher.) Read out loud to the class the data points from lowest to highest for each of the top six occupations. The students are expected to record the bid information as you read out loud. Allow approximately 30 minutes for the students to complete Activity 9.2.

7. Call the group together and discuss the following:
   a. Which occupation has the highest bid? (Answers will vary.)
   b. Which occupation has the lowest bid? (Answers will vary.)
   c. Which occupation had the largest number of bids? (Answers will vary.)
   d. Which occupation had the greatest range of values? (Answers will vary.)
   e. Which occupation had the greatest interquartile range? (Answers will vary.)
   f. Which occupation seems to have the most variability in the data? (Answers will vary.)
   g. Do the box and whisker plots for each occupation look similar? (Answers will vary.)
   h. I am sure many of you are wondering whom you ended up with for your team. First let me hand back your original bids (Activity 9.1). I will now announce the top bids for each occupation and the team that made the bid. Please keep track of the team members you and your partner were able to obtain. (Read the top bid for each occupation and the corresponding team letter.)
   i. Did any of you fill your team? (Acknowledge teams that met their goals.) We have some occupations left over. Would any of you be interested in them? (Offer some of the occupations that received few if any bids, such as the talk show host or the banker.)
   j. Why are you NOT interested in these occupations for your team? (They don't have the skills necessary for survival on a deserted island.)
   k. Given the situation of a deserted island, some occupations are not as highly valued as other occupations. In the situation of surviving a deserted island, some occupations are not valued and some are highly prized. Which occupation is the least prized on the island? (Record on the board.) Which occupation is the most prized? (Record on the board.)

Closure

1. Assign Activity 9.3. Allow 10 minutes to complete. Review student responses.

2. Conclude the lesson by stating that not all occupations are created equal and the value of an occupation depends very highly on the situation. Tell the group that they will have the opportunity to investigate this concept in future lessons.

Extensions

It would be interesting for the students to compare actual salary information for the occupations on Activity 9.1 and evaluate how the information affects the box and whisker plots.

ACTIVITY 9.1

Team _____

Select Your All-Star Team
For Surviving a Deserted Island

Instructions

You and your partner have the task of selecting up to five people to survive on a deserted, primitive, and completely isolated island. You have a budget of $150,000 to spend on these five people. Select carefully, as your lives will depend on it. You and your partner are in a bidding war with the rest of the class to put together a team to help you survive on the island. There are 24 occupations listed in the table below. The number in parentheses represents the number of workers for each occupation. Your job is to choose up to five people from the listing of occupations and stay within your budget of $150,000.

Occupation	Occupation	Occupation	Occupation	Occupation	Occupation
Talk Show Host (2)	Science Teacher (2)	Computer Programmer (2)	Movie Star (2)	Farmer (2)	Stock Broker (2)
Occupation	**Occupation**	**Occupation**	**Occupation**	**Occupation**	**Occupation**
Mechanic (2)	Airline Pilot (2)	Drummer(2)	Police Officer (2)	Family Counselor (2)	Cook (2)
Occupation	**Occupation**	**Occupation**	**Occupation**	**Occupation**	**Occupation**
Inventor (2)	Banker (2)	Sales Manager (2)	Engineer (2)	Housewife (2)	Fishing Guide (2)
Occupation	**Occupation**	**Occupation**	**Occupation**	**Occupation**	**Occupation**
Carpenter (2)	Nurse (2)	Stand Up Comic (2)	NBA Star (2)	Navy Seal (2)	Wedding Planner (2)

List your top picks in order from highest to lowest and the amount of each bid. Remember, you have $150,000 to spend on the entire team. You may not spend more than $150,000 in total.

Occupation	Bid Amount
#1_____	$_____
#2_____	$_____
#3_____	$_____
#4_____	$_____
#5_____	$_____
TOTAL	$_____

 Mathematics and Economics: Connections for Life © National Council on Economic Education, New York, NY

ACTIVITY 9.2 ▲ Box and Whisker Data Summary

1. Record the bid data for the top six occupations in the space below. Arrange the bids in order from least to greatest.

Occupations	Bid Data (Arranged from Lowest to Highest)
1.	
2.	
3.	
4.	
5.	
6.	

2. To set up a box and whisker plot you will need to calculate five pieces of data: the lowest value, the highest value, the median, the lower quartile, and the upper quartile. The data set below will be used as an example to help you complete steps a-d.

   18,27,34,52,54,59,61,68,78,82,85,87,91,93,100

   a) Record the lowest and highest bid for each occupation in the table below. *(18 and 100)*

   b) Find the median for each occupation and record it in the table below. The median is the value exactly in the middle of the data set. *(68)* If there is an even number of bids, you will use the average of the two middle numbers.

   c) Find the median of the lower half of the bid data and record it in the table below. The lower half median, called the lower quartile, is the value exactly in the middle of the bids to the left of the median. *(52)*

   d) Find the median of the upper half of the bid data and record it in the table below. The upper half median, called the upper quartile, is the value exactly in the middle of the bids to the right of the median. *(87)*

Occupations	Lowest Value	Highest Value	Median	Lower Quartile	Upper Quartile
Example	18	100	68	52	87
1.					
2.					
3.					
4.					
5.					
6.					

3. With the data from the chart above, you will create a box and whisker plot for each occupation. A box and whisker plot is easy to construct. Just follow the example below and create your own plot.

   a) From the previous example data in number 2 you have the five pieces of data necessary to construct the box and whisker plot. First plot the **minimum value** (18) and the **maximum value** (100).

   b) Plot the **median** (68).

   c) Plot the **lower** and **upper quartile** values (52, 87).

   d) Now you are ready to create the box. Draw a small rectangle that starts at the lower quartile value and ends at the upper quartile value. What is the distance between the upper and lower quartile values? This distance is called the **interquartile range**.

   e) Now you're ready to add the whiskers to the plot. Draw a straight line between the minimum value and the lower quartile and a straight line between the maximum value and the upper quartile. Your box should look similar to the example.

5. Use the chart on the next page to create a box and whisker plot for the top six occupations.

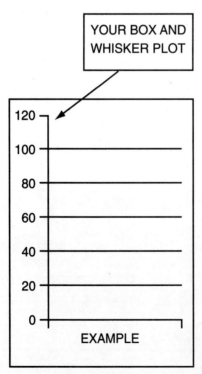

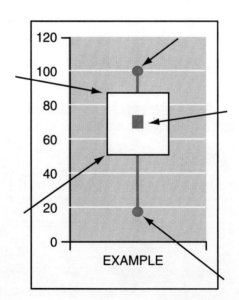

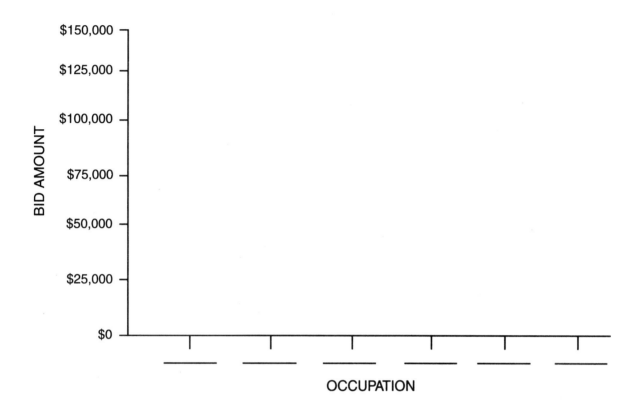

ACTIVITY 9.3 ▲ Are All Occupations Created Equal?

1. Complete the table below using the same list of occupations from Activity 9.1.

Situation	Least Prized Occupation	Most Prized Occupation	Most Valuable Skill	Least Valuable Skill
Stranded on a deserted island				

2. Write one or two sentences that summarize the information in the table above; you must use the words "value," "occupation," and "situation" in the summary.

3. Complete the table below, using the same list of occupations from Activity 9.1; note the change in situation.

Situation	Least Prized Occupation	Most Prized Occupation	Most Valuable Skill	Least Valuable Skill
Operating a successful business				

4. Write one or two sentences that summarize the information in the table above; you must use the words "value," "occupation," and "situation" in the summary.

5. Are all occupations created equal? Why not?

6. How can a box and whisker plot clearly summarize data?

If you were stranded
on a deserted island,
WHOM would you want
there with you?

VISUAL 9.2

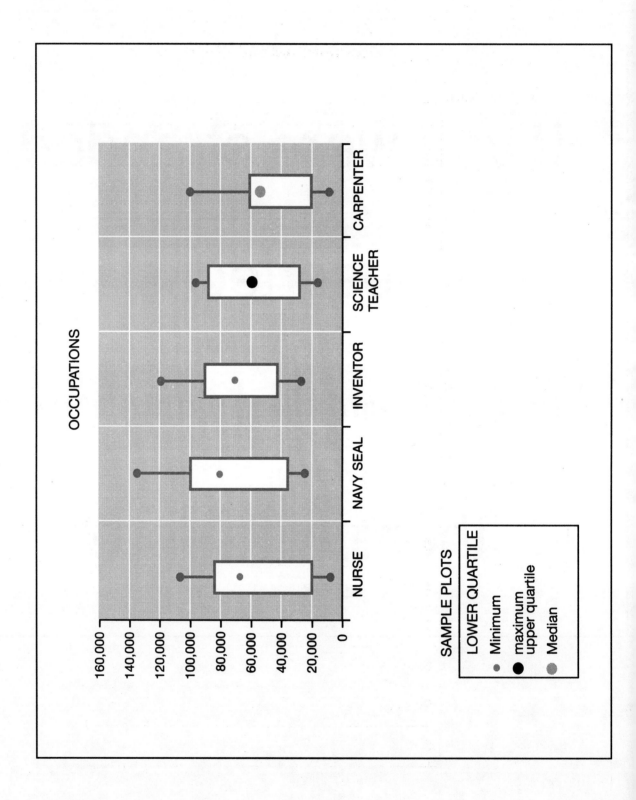

Occupational Bid Sheet

Occupation: _____

Bid	Team
$	
$	
$	
$	
$	
$	
$	
$	
$	
$	
$	
$	
$	
$	
$	

Where Does the Price of Pizza Come From? Part 1

Mathematics Prerequisites

Prior to this lesson, students should know:
➤ Coordinate system.
➤ Slope.
➤ Y-intercept.
➤ Point-slope form of an equation.

Lesson Objectives

Students will be able to:
➤ Graph tabular data and from that data write the equation for a straight line.
➤ Compare and contrast two specific linear functions.
➤ Find the solution for two linear equations.
➤ Define market, supply, demand, and equilibrium.

Abstract

This lesson challenges students to identify the source of market prices. The students will complete a series of activities that represent supply and demand. In Activity 10.1, the students are asked to plot points, connect the points through a straight line, and write the equation for the line. The two sets of data represent supply and demand for pizza in the small town of Pizzaville. In Activity 10.2, the students compare and contrast the two linear equations. Finally, in Activity 10.3, the students combine the supply and demand curves to find the intersection point and identify that point as the market price. The formal terms of supply, demand, and equilibrium are introduced.

Mathematics Terms

➤ Coordinate points
➤ Linear function
➤ Graphs
➤ Tables

Materials

➤ One copy of Activities 10.1, 10.2, and 10.3 for each student
➤ Transparencies of Visuals 10.1–10.5.

Estimated Time

One class period

Warm-Up Activities

Problem 1

Taxi prices in a medium size town are $2.00 for the start-up fee and $1.00 per mile after that. Make a table showing the cost for 5 miles, 10 miles and 15 miles.

Miles:	5	10	15
Price:	$7.00	$12.00	$17.00

Use the information from your table to graph the data on a coordinate graph. Let the price be on the y-axis and the miles be on the x-axis. (Show first graph on Visual 10.1.) Determine the equation of the line in the slope-intercept form. [y = (x) + 2] Determine the slope of the line and the y-intercept. (The slope is 1 and the y-intercept is $2.00.)

Problem 2

At a baseball stadium the vendors start out with 24,000 hot dogs. They know they will sell about 4,000 during each 30-minute segment of the game. Make a table showing the decline in the number of hot dogs in thousands as the game goes on until there are no hot dogs left.

Number of hot dogs:	20,000	16,000	12,000	8,000	4,000
Time (from start of game)	30 min	60 min	90 min	120 min	150 min

Put your information on a coordinate graph with the number of hot dogs on the y-axis (in thousands) and the time on the x-axis.

Use the information from your table to graph the data on a coordinate graph. (Show second graph on Visual 10.1.) Determine the equation of the line in the slope-intercept form. [y=(-4,000/30)(x) + 24,000]

Determine the slope of the line and the y-intercept. (The slope is –4,000/30 and the y-intercept is 24,000.)

Procedures

1. Display Visual 10.2. Discuss the following:
    a. Raise your hand if you have eaten pizza in the last week. Wow! Many of you have been eating pizza. What price did you pay? (Record prices on the board.)

b. Where do you suppose the price for the pizza came from? (Record some student responses on the board.)

c. We will begin our investigation into where and how prices are generated. Today you will begin the investigation by looking at some data related to pizza prices. You will graph two sets of data and write the equations for these two data sets. You will also learn some new vocabulary terms to describe the data you are investigating.

2. Distribute a copy of Activity 10.1 to each student. Review the directions for the activity, and provide the students with approximately 15 minutes to complete the activity.

3. Call the group back together and discuss the following:

a. Let's look at the results of your graphing. Could I have a volunteer to graph Part A on one half of the board and another volunteer to graph Part B on the other half of the board? (Check these graphs for accuracy. They are also reproduced as Visual 10.3.)

b. Okay, who can give me the equation for Graph A and Graph B? Please come up and write the appropriate equation next to the appropriate graph. [y = (1/250)(x) and y = 20 − (1/250)(x)]

4. Distribute a copy of Activity 10.2 to each student. Review the directions for the activity and provide the students with approximately 10 minutes to complete the activity.

5. Call the group back together and discuss their responses.

Seller's Graph	Buyer's Graph
1. y = (1/250)(x)	1. y = 20 − (1/250)(x)
2. 0	2. 20
3. $18	3. $2
4. Direct relationship. Higher the price, more sellers are willing to sell.	4. Inverse relationship. Lower the price, more buyers are willing to buy.

6. Announce that we are still trying to answer the question of where pizza prices come from and Activity 10.3 will offer the solution.

7. Distribute a copy of Activity 10.3 to each student. Review the directions and provide approximately 10 minutes for the activity.

8. Call the group back together and discuss the results. Ask for two students to each graph the buyer's and seller's line and determine the intersection. Ask another student to label the three vocabulary words on the graph.

9. Display Visual 10.4. Ask the students to respond to this question. Check for accuracy of responses. (Prices come from the interaction of buyers and sellers in the marketplace or prices come from the intersection of supply and demand.)

10. Announce that students will continue their work with market prices in another lesson.

Extensions

1. Students can survey local pizza establishments to determine selling prices for large, two-topping pizzas in their own town.

2. Students can survey their classmates to determine local demand for large, two-topping pizzas.

3. Students may explore the use of systems of equations method to solve for the market price of pizza in Pizzaville.

ACTIVITY 10.1

Let's look at a typical American town where people enjoy pizza as much as you guys do. We will call the town Pizzaville. We will be examining prices for large, two-topping pizzas. You will work with two sets of data on this worksheet, one representing Pizzaville sellers and the other, Pizzaville buyers. Table A contains the data for pizza sellers and Table B contains data for pizza buyers. Follow the instructions below and be prepared to share your results.

Table A

Pizza Price	Number of Pizzas
$18	4,500
$16	4,000
$14	3,500
$12	3,000
$10	2,500
$ 8	2,000
$ 6	1,500
$ 4	1,000
$ 2	500

1. Using the chart below, plot the points from Table A. Connect the points to form a line. Write the equation for the line in the space provided.

Equation for the line: _____

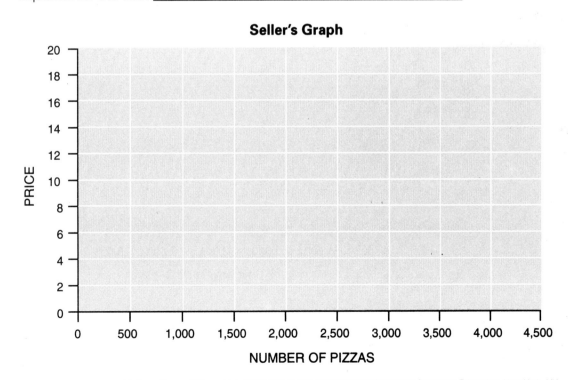

Seller's Graph

ACTIVITY 10.1 (continued)

2. Using the chart below, plot the points from Table B. Connect the points to form a line. Write the equation for the line in the space provided.

Equation for the line: _____

Table B

Pizza Price	Number of Pizzas Sold
$18	500
$16	1,000
$14	1,500
$12	2,000
$10	2,500
$ 8	3,000
$ 6	3,500
$ 4	4,000
$ 2	4,500

Buyer's Graph

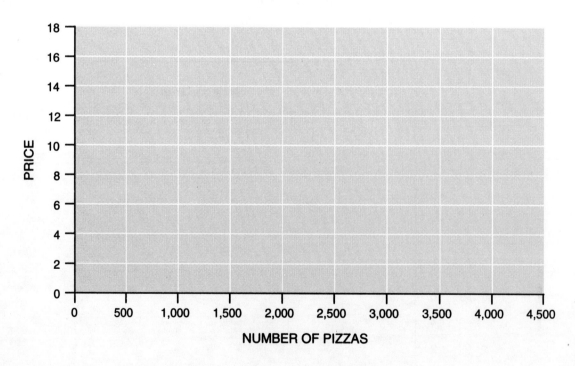

ACTIVITY 10.1 (continued)

3. What group of people is represented by the Table A data?

   _____

4. What group of people is represented by the Table B data?

   _____

ACTIVITY 10.2

Compare and contrast the Seller's Graph (data from Table A) with the Buyer's Graph (data from Table B). Complete questions 1-4 in the table below for both the Seller's Graph and the Buyer's Graph. Put your answers in the appropriate box. Now use the sections on the far right to make notes about the similarities and differences between the graphs in terms of their characteristics. Your goal in completing this chart is to determine what the slope for the Seller's and Buyer's lines have in common and how they are different.

	Items to be Compared		
Characteristics	**#1. Seller's Graph**	**#2. Buyer's Graph**	**Compare and Contrast**
1. What is the slope of the line?			Similarities Differences
2. What is the y-intercept?			Similarities Differences
3. At what price are buyers/sellers willing to buy/sell the most?			Similarities Differences
4. What can be said about price of pizza and the number of pizzas people are willing to sell or buy?			Similarities Differences

Write a summary statement of what you have learned about the Sellers and Buyers in the Pizzaville pizza market.

ACTIVITY 10.3

Our original question today asked where the price of pizza came from, and the answer to that question involves both the buyers and sellers of pizza. When buyers and sellers come together and exchange goods and services, we call that interaction a market. In Pizzaville we have buyers and sellers exchanging pizzas, so we have a market. Can you find the market price for a large, two-topping pizza in Pizzaville? Solve the mystery of where pizza prices came from by combining your graphs of Table A and Table B. Use the graph below to plot the points from Table A and Table B.

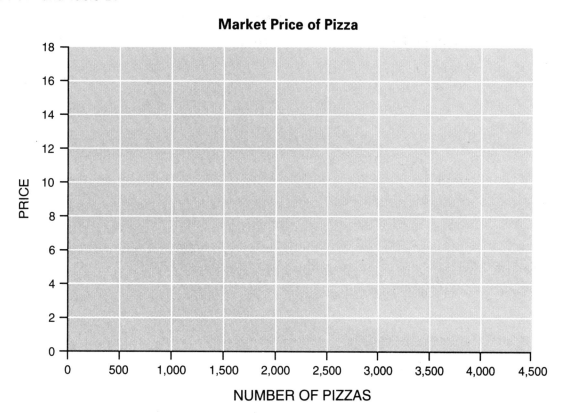

Market Price of Pizza

The market price of pizza comes from the intersection of your buyer and seller graphs. At what price do these two graphs intersect? _____

1. There are three important vocabulary words for you to associate with the graph above and they are *supply, demand,* and *equilibrium.* Write "supply" next to the upward sloping Seller's line because that line represents how much and at what price sellers will supply pizzas to the town of Pizzaville. Write "demand" next to the downward sloping Buyer's line because that line represents how much and at what price buyers are willing to buy pizzas. Finally, write "equilibrium" next to the intersection of the Supply and Demand lines because where the two lines cross is where the price and quantity between buyers and sellers is equal. Equilibrium, where the two lines intersect, is where the price of pizza comes from.

2. Write a summary statement about the intersecting lines in the graph above using the words *supply, demand, equilibrium,* and *price.*

VISUAL 10.1 ▲ Answers to Warm-Up

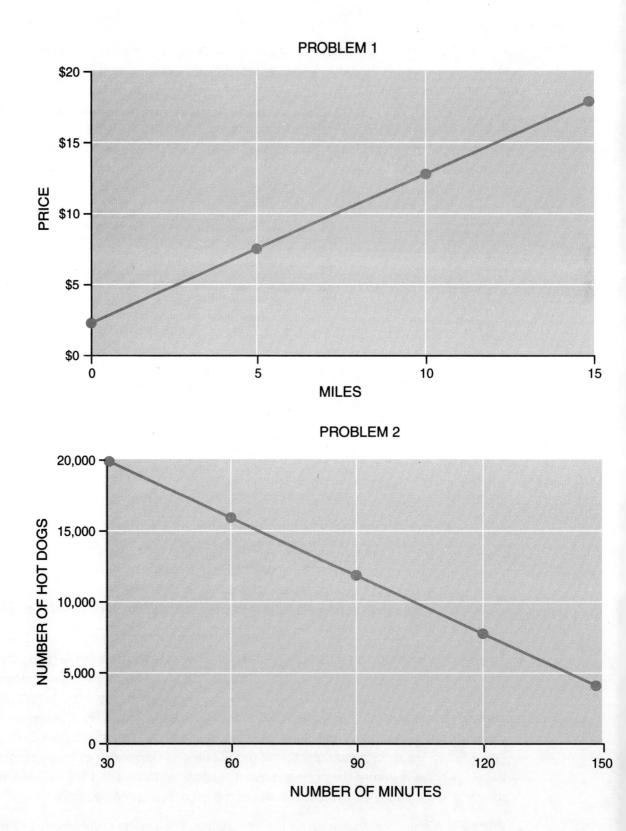

PROBLEM 1

PRICE vs. MILES

PROBLEM 2

NUMBER OF HOT DOGS vs. NUMBER OF MINUTES

WHERE DOES THE PRICE OF PIZZA COME FROM?

1. Using the chart below, plot the points from Table A. Connect the points to form a line. Write the equation for the line in the space provided. **Equation for the line:** y = (1/250)(x)

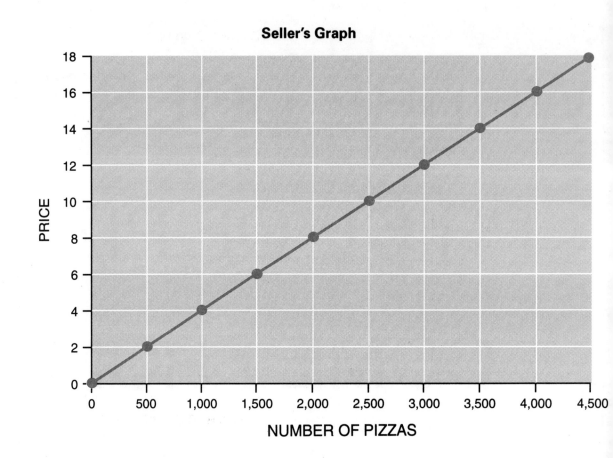

Seller's Graph

PRICE

NUMBER OF PIZZAS

2. Using the chart below, plot the points from Table B. Connect the points to form a line. Write the equation for the line in the space provided. **Equation for the line:** $y = (-1/250)(x) + 20$

Buyer's Graph

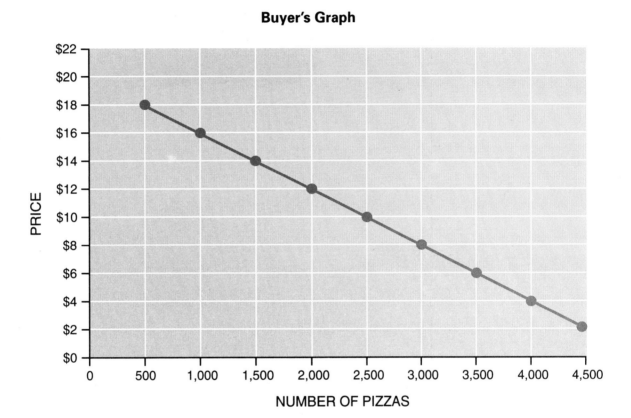

NUMBER OF PIZZAS

3. What group of people is represented by Table A data? Sellers

4. What group is represented by Table B data? Buyers

Compare and contrast the Seller's Graph (data from Table A) with the Buyer's Graph (data from Table B). Complete questions 1-4 in the table below for both the Seller's Graph and the Buyer's Graph. Put your answers in the appropriate box. Now use the sections on the far right to make notes about the similarities and differences between the graphs in terms of their characteristics. Your goal in completing this chart is to determine what the slope for the Seller's and Buyer's lines have in common and how they are different.

	Items to be Compared		
Characteristics	**#1. Seller's Graph**	**#2. Buyer's Graph**	**Compare and Contrast**
1. What is the slope of the line?	1/250	– 1/250	Similarities Same denominator Same numerator Differences Different sign
2. What is the y-intercept?	0	20	Similarities Neither are negative Differences Different numbers
3. At what price are buyers/sellers willing to buy/sell the most?	$18	$2	Similarities Both groups use money Differences Buyers want to spend little, sellers want to sell for a lot.
4. What can be said about price of pizza and the number of pizzas people are willing to sell or buy?	At high prices, sellers are willing to offer the most number of pizzas.	At low prices, buyers are willing to purchase the most number of pizzas.	Similarities None Differences Each group wants the opposite type of price, buyers low and sellers high.

Write a summary statement of what you have learned about the Sellers and Buyers in the Pizzaville pizza market. Buyers are looking to spend as little as possible for pizza and sellers are looking to sell at as high a price as possible.

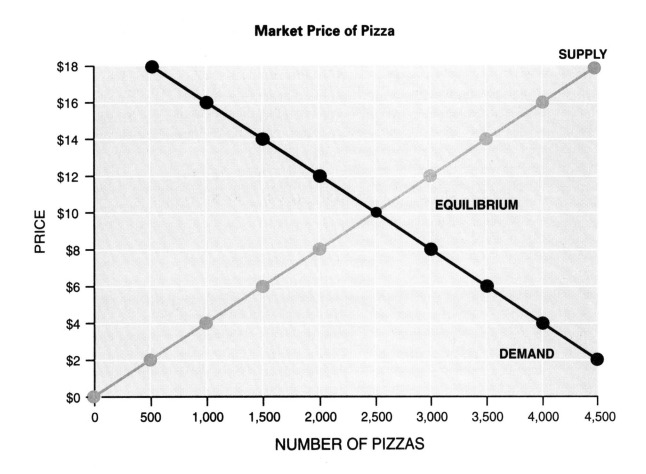

Market Price of Pizza

Where Does the Price of Pizza Come From? Part 2

Mathematics Prerequisites

Prior to this lesson, students should know:
- Coordinate system.
- Slope.
- Y-intercept.
- Point-slope form of an equation.

Economics Prerequisites

- Demand
- Supply
- Equilibrium

Lesson Objectives

Students will be able to:
- Shift linear equations.
- Graphically solve systems of linear equations.
- Predict price movement in a market setting.
- Recognize that price is a dynamic mechanism responding to changes in the marketplace.

Abstract

In this lesson students continue to examine where prices come from (see Lesson 10), applying the concepts of *supply*, *demand*, and *equilibrium*. Students will examine changes within a market for pizza utilizing linear equations as the vehicle for examining shifting supply and demand equations. Transformation of linear equations and calculating the new intersection will provide students with the framework for exploring the dynamics of a market.

Mathematics Terms

- Coordinate points
- Linear function
- Graphs
- Tables

Materials

- One copy of Activities 11.1 and 11.2 for each student
- One copy of Activities 11.3 and 11.4 for each quarter of the class

➤ Transparencies of Visuals 11.1–11.5
➤ Price Change Cards: front and back

Estimated Time

Two class periods

Warm-Up Activity

1. Martha has a van rental shop. She rents SUVs by the week. Her basic charge is $320.00 per week plus $.20 per mile.

   a. Graph the price for renting a SUV for one week and driving 500 miles. Put the miles on the x-axis (use 100-mile increments) and put the price on the y-axis. Identify the slope and the y-intercept of the line, and write the equation of the line. (Slope is 1/5, y-intercept is $320, and the equation is y = (1/5)(x) + 320. Graphs for a, b, and c can be found on Visual 11.1.)

   b. Suppose Martha wishes to increase her income. Her choices are to raise the initial charge or raise the per-mile charge. On your graph, graph the effect of raising the initial fee by $50.00 (without raising the per-mile charge). Identify the slope, y-intercept, and the equation of the line. (Slope 1/5, y-intercept is $370, and the equation is y = (1/5)(x) + 370.)

   c. Now on the same graph, graph the effect of raising the per-mile fee to $.30 per mile. Again, identify the slope, y-intercept, and the equation of the new line. (Slope is 3/10, y-intercept is $320, and the equation is y = (3/10)(x) + 320.)

   d. What would your recommendation for increased income be and why? (Answers will vary.)

Procedures

1. Display Visual 11.2. Discuss the following:

   a. Does this graph look familiar? It should, because this is the graph you created just the other day. Who can review for us what the data represent? (Select a volunteer.)

   b. What do the data along the vertical axis represent? (Price of pizza.) What do the data along the horizontal axis represent? (Number of pizzas.)

   c. If you recall, we used two sets of data to create the linear graphs. Do you remember the group that is represented by the downward sloping line? (Buyers of pizza.) What official label did we use for this line? (Demand.) Label the Demand line.

   d. Do you remember the group that is represented by the upward sloping line? (Sellers of pizza.) What official label did we use for this line? (Supply.) Label the Supply line.

   e. In the previous lesson, you were asked to solve for the intersection of the supply and demand lines. What did we call that intersection?

(Equilibrium. Draw a large dot to locate equilibrium. Then, using a dashed line, connect horizontally the dot at equilibrium with the price of $10. Use another dashed line to connect vertically the dot at equilibrium down to the quantity of 2,500 pizzas.)

f. At the intersection of supply and demand, at equilibrium, 2,500 pizzas will be sold at a price of $10.

g. In the previous lesson, we asked where prices come from. We determined that price involves both buyers and sellers and that we could determine a market price at the intersection of supply and demand.

h. Today, we want to examine this idea of where price comes from and give you some practice determining price and predicting changes in price. Your job today will be to determine, using your math knowledge and some economic know-how, the direction, up or down, of pizza prices.

2. Distribute Activity 11.1 and review the directions. Allow 10 minutes to complete the activity.

3. Discuss Activity 11.1. Ask for volunteers to graph S2 and S3. Be sure to reinforce the idea that the equilibrium price decreases when supply is increased. (Answers to Activity 11.1 can be found in Visual 11.3.) *(Holding demand constant.)* Collect Activity 11.1. (Be sure students put their names on the activity sheets.)

4. Announce that students will now manipulate the buyer side of the market, the Demand line. Distribute Activity 11.2 and review the directions. Allow 10 minutes for completion.

5. Discuss Activity 11.2. Ask for volunteers to graph D2 and D3. Be sure to reinforce the idea that the equilibrium price decreases when demand is reduced. (Answers to Activity 11.2 can be found in Visual 11.4.) *(Holding supply constant.)* Collect Activity 11.2. (Be sure students put their names on the activity sheets.)

6. Announce that the class will now examine a market for lawn mowing services in Pizzaville. Display Visual 11.5. Ask for a volunteer to identify supply, demand, and equilibrium. Identify the equilibrium price ($45) and number of lawns mowed (100).

7. Designate half of the room to work on supply and the other half to work on demand. Place the students into groups of two. Distribute Activity 11.3 to the supply group and Activity 11.4 to the demand group. Review the instructions. Assign each pair of students to either increase or decrease the data on their handout. Allow 15 minutes for completion.

8. Once the students have completed their shifts, distribute a *Price Change Card* to each pair of students. Instruct the students in each

group to write their names at the top of the card and to fill in their story line on the front of the card. They are NOT to write on the back of the card yet. Collect all the cards.

9. Redistribute one *Price Change Card* to each group. Check to make sure that no group receives its own original card. Instruct each group to read the story line on the front of the card and to answer questions 1-3 on the back of the *Price Change Card.*

10. Announce that we will now see how well everyone predicted changes in price. Ask for volunteers to share the names of the authors on their cards and to read the story line. *(As an example: "This is Tanya and Joey's story and it states. . .")* Ask if the story represents supply or demand, and ask the students to share their prediction on the change in equilibrium price. Record this information on the board. For example:

Story Line   Supply or Demand   Prediction of Increase or Decrease in Equilibrium Price

11. Ask the authors of the story line if they agree. (Hopefully yes!) Announce that the class will determine whether the price prediction is correct. Ask the authors to record their data points on the board.

12. Display Visual 11.5. Plot the author's data points on Visual 11.5. *(This line could represent either supply or demand. Label the new line either D2 or S2).* Draw a line to connect the points and identify the intersection of D1-S2 or S1-D2, depending on whether the example shifted supply or demand. Announce the change in price, either up or down, as confirmed by the graphs. *Congratulate or gently correct the pair of students whose prediction was used.*

13. Announce that together we will check the accuracy of everyone's predictions. Ask each pair of students to take responsibility for either their *Price Change Card* or their activity. *(Either Activity 11.3 or Activity 11.4).*

14. Announce that the students will help you organize the *Price Change Cards* and the Activity by matching up the student names on both documents. As an example, Tanya and Joey have both a story line card and Activity 11.3 or 11.4. Ask the students to match the story line student names with the student names on the activity. Once they have the match, instruct the students to staple the two documents together and turn them in to you.

15. Settle everyone down and announce the following:
   a. Prices in the marketplace do not always stay the same. We often

    see the number of buyers and sellers change; when that happens, the equilibrium price can also change.

  b. A shift in the supply or demand line causes changes in the equilibrium price of the goods and services.

  c. So, where do equilibrium prices come from? (They come from the interaction of buyers and sellers.)

  d. Do prices stay the same over time? (No. Prices change when the number of buyers and sellers changes.)

  e. Can we predict the direction of price changes? (Yes, if we know how the number of buyers or sellers is changing.)

  f. If time allows, the students can check the accuracy of the predictions by comparing the information in Activities 11.3 and 11.4 with the corresponding *Price Change Cards,* as the group did in step 12.

Extensions

1. As an assignment, the students could algebraically solve the systems of equations for each story line.

2. The students could survey their local market for actual lawn mowing prices and determine if there is any trend, up or down, in the price of lawn mowing.

ACTIVITY 11.1 ▲ Change in Supply

1. At $10 for a large, two-topping pizza, two pizza makers from the neighboring town figure they can make good money selling pizzas in Pizzaville. To simplify things, we will say that the number of pizzas offered for sale will increase by exactly 1,000 pizzas at each price. Fill in the number of pizzas in Table A below for Supply 2 and plot the new supply line next to the original supply line. Label the new supply line "S2."

2. The equation for the original supply line is y = (1/250)(x). Find the equation for S2.
   S2 equation: _____

3. Let's take another look at how the number of pizzas might increase as a result of new sellers entering the Pizzaville market. In this case, the number of pizzas increases by exactly 50% at each price. Fill in the number of pizzas in Table A for Supply 3. Plot the new supply line and label it S3. **S3 equation**: _____

Table A

Price of Pizza	Supply 1	Supply 2	Supply 3
$18	4,500	5,500	6,750
$16	4,000		
$14	3,500		
$12	3,000		
$10	2,500		
$ 8	2,000		
$ 6	1,500		
$ 4	1,000		
$ 2	500		

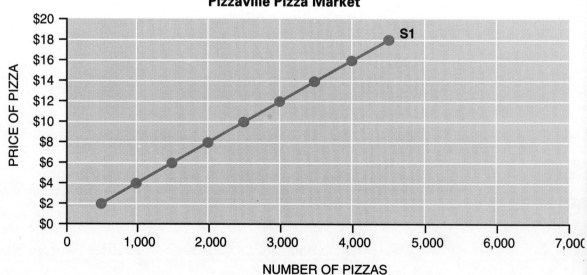

Pizzaville Pizza Market

4. In order to find the price of pizza in Pizzaville you will need to include the buyer's side of the market. Graph the demand line using the following ordered pairs: (4500, $2), (4000, $4), (3500, $6), (3000, $8), (2500, $10), (2000, $12), (1500, $14), (1000, $16), (500, $18). Using S1 and D1, the equilibrium price is _____ and the equilibrium number of pizzas is _____. Using S2 and D1, the equilibrium price is _____ and the equilibrium number of pizzas is _____. Using S3 and D1, the equilibrium price is _____ and the equilibrium number of pizzas is_____.

Compare and contrast S1, S2, S3. Complete the table below for the three supply lines. Put your answers in the appropriate boxes; then use the sections on the far right to make notes about the similarities and differences between the graphs in terms of their characteristics.

Characteristics	Items to be Compared			Compare and Contrast
	S1	S2	S3	
5. What is the slope of the line?				Similarities Differences
6. What is the y-intercept?				Similarities Differences
7. For S2 and S3, what words were used to indicate the amount of change in each supply line? What aspect of the equation changed?				Similarities Differences
8. What change took place when the number of pizza sellers in Pizzaville increased?				Similarities Differences

9. How did increasing the number of sellers change the equilibrium price of pizza?

10. Write a summary statement of what you have learned about the three supply lines in the Pizzaville pizza market.

ACTIVITY 11.2 ▲ Change in Demand

1. The city of Pizzaville decided to promote healthy eating for its residents by sponsoring a weight-loss program that offered awards to anyone who could lose ten pounds over the next three months. The effect of this program has caused some changes in the number of pizzas that people are willing to buy in Pizzaville. To keep things simple, we will say that the number of pizzas that people will buy will decrease by exactly 1,000 pizzas at each price. Fill in the number of pizzas in Table B below for Demand 2, and plot the new demand line next to the original demand line. Label the new demand "D2."

2. The equation for the original demand line is $y = 20 - (1/250)(x)$. Find the equation for D2. **The D2 equation is:** _____

3. Let's take another look at how the number of pizzas might decrease as a result of people buying fewer pizzas. In this case, the number of pizzas decreases by exactly 75% at each price. Fill in the number of pizzas in Table B below for Demand 3. Plot the new demand line and label it D3. **The D3 equation is** _____

Table B

Price of Pizza	Demand 1	Demand 2	Demand 3
$18	500	−500	125
$16	1,000		
$14	1,500		
$12	2,000		
$10	2,500		
$ 8	3,000		
$ 6	3,500		
$ 4	4,000		
$ 2	4,500		

ACTIVITY 11.2 (continued)

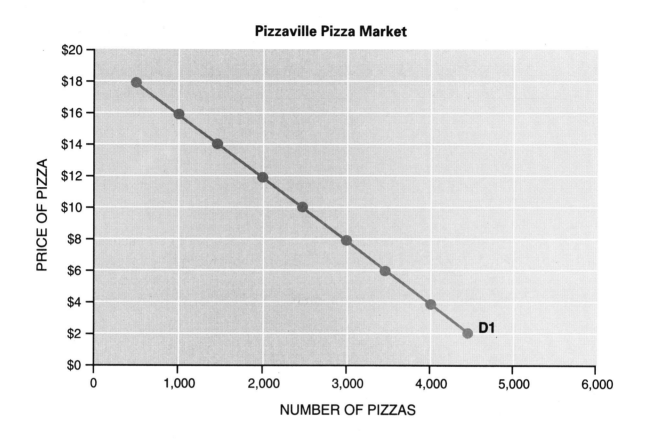

Pizzaville Pizza Market

PRICE OF PIZZA (y-axis): $0, $2, $4, $6, $8, $10, $12, $14, $16, $18, $20

NUMBER OF PIZZAS (x-axis): 0, 1,000, 2,000, 3,000, 4,000, 5,000, 6,000

D1

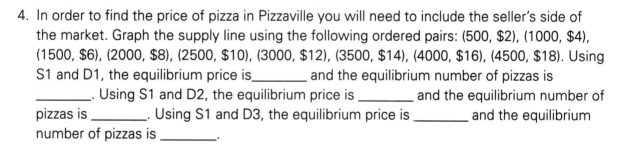

4. In order to find the price of pizza in Pizzaville you will need to include the seller's side of the market. Graph the supply line using the following ordered pairs: (500, $2), (1000, $4), (1500, $6), (2000, $8), (2500, $10), (3000, $12), (3500, $14), (4000, $16), (4500, $18). Using S1 and D1, the equilibrium price is_____ and the equilibrium number of pizzas is _____. Using S1 and D2, the equilibrium price is _____ and the equilibrium number of pizzas is _____. Using S1 and D3, the equilibrium price is _____ and the equilibrium number of pizzas is _____.

Compare and contrast D1, D2, D3. Complete questions 1-4 in the table below for the three supply lines from questions 4 and 5. Put your answers in the appropriate boxes; then use the sections on the far right to make notes about the similarities and differences between the graphs in terms of their characteristics.

Characteristics	Items to be Compared			Compare and Contrast
	S1	S2	S3	
5. What is the slope of the line?				Similarities Differences
6. What is the y-intercept?				Similarities Differences
7. For S2 and S3, what words were used to indicate the amount of change in each supply line? What aspect of the equation changed?				Similarities Differences
8. What change took place when people were less willing to buy less pizza in order to lose weight?				Similarities Differences

9. How did decreasing the number of pizzas people wanted to buy change the equilibrium price of pizza?

10. Write a summary statement of what you have learned about the three demand lines in the Pizzaville pizza market.

ACTIVITY 11.3 ▲ Change in Supply

Student Names: _____ and _____

You and your partner are going to cause a change in the number of lawns mowed in Pizzaville. You must come up with a story line that will affect the number of lawns mowed at each price level. Your teacher will assign you to increase or decrease the number of lawns mowed.

Circle the type of change you will cause: INCREASE   or   DECREASE

The change you create can be a constant amount added to or subtracted from the number of lawns at each price, or you can apply a percentage increase or decrease. Follow the directions below to create your story line and data points. Be prepared to share your story, data points, and the equation for your shift in supply.

1. In two sentences or less, create a reason why the number of lawns mowed will increase or decrease at each price. Think about what might actually cause this type of change and include the word "sellers."

   _____

   _____

2. Select a specific amount by which the number of lawns mowed will increase or decrease.

   INCREASE by a constant of_____ or by _____%

   DECREASE by a constant of _____ or by _____%

3. Fill in the data points in Table 1 below. Plot the points and label the new supply line S2. The equation for S2 is: _____. The equilibrium price is _____ and number of lawns mowed is _____.

Price	S1	S2
$75	160	
$60	130	
$45	100	
$30	70	
$15	40	

ACTIVITY 11.3 (continued)

In order to find the equilibrium price of lawn mowing in Pizzaville, you will need to include the buyer's side of the market. Graph the demand line using the following ordered pairs: (40, $75), (70, $60), (100, $45), (130, $30), (160, $15). (See Visual 11.5) Using S1 and D1, the equilibrium price is _____ and the equilibrium number of yards mowed is _____. Using S1 and D2, the equilibrium price is _____ and the equilibrium number of yards mowed is _____.

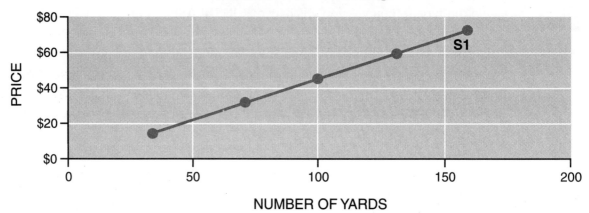

Market for Lawn Mowing

ACTIVITY 11.4 ▲ Change in Demand

Student Names: _____ and _____

You and your partner are going to cause a change in the number of times people have their lawns mowed in Pizzaville. You must come up with a story line that will affect the number of lawns mowed at each price level. Your teacher will assign you to increase or decrease the number of lawns mowed.

Circle the type of change you will cause: INCREASE   or   DECREASE

The change you create can be a constant amount added to or subtracted from the number of lawns at each price, or you can apply a percentage increase or decrease. Follow the directions below to create your story line and data points. Be prepared to share your story, data points, and the equation for your shift in supply.

1. In two sentences or less, create a reason why the number of lawns people want to have mowed will increase or decrease at each price. Think about what might actually cause this type of change and include the word "buyers."

   _____

   _____

2. Select a specific amount by which the number of lawns mowed will increase or decrease.

   INCREASE by a constant of_____ or by _____%

   DECREASE by a constant of _____ or by _____%

3. Fill in the data points in Table 1 below. Plot the points and label the new supply line D2. The equation for D2 is: _____. The equilibrium price is _____ and number of lawns mowed is _____.

Price	D1	D2
$75	40	
$60	70	
$45	100	
$30	130	
$15	160	

In order to find the equilibrium price of lawn mowing in Pizzaville, you will need to include the seller's side of the market. Graph the supply line using the following ordered pairs: (160, $75), (130, $60), (100, $45), (70, $30), (40, $15). (See Visual 11.5) Using S1 and D1, the equilibrium price is _____ and the equilibrium number of yards mowed is _____. Using S1 and D2, the equilibrium price is _____ and the equilibrium number of yards mowed is _____.

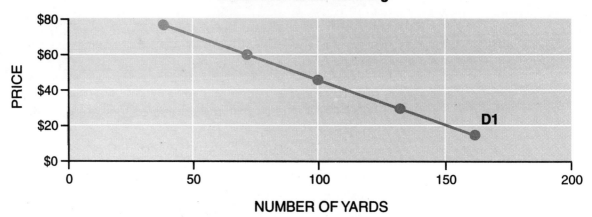

Market for Lawn Mowing

VISUAL 11.1

MARTHA's SUV RATES: WARM-UP #1a

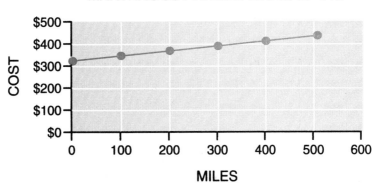

MARTHA's SUV RATES: WARM-UP #1b

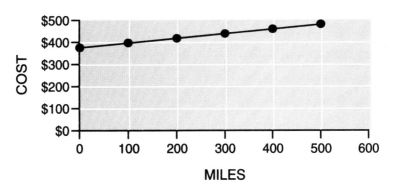

MARTHA's SUV RATES: WARM-UP #1b & #1c

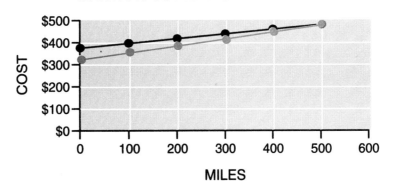

VISUAL 11.2

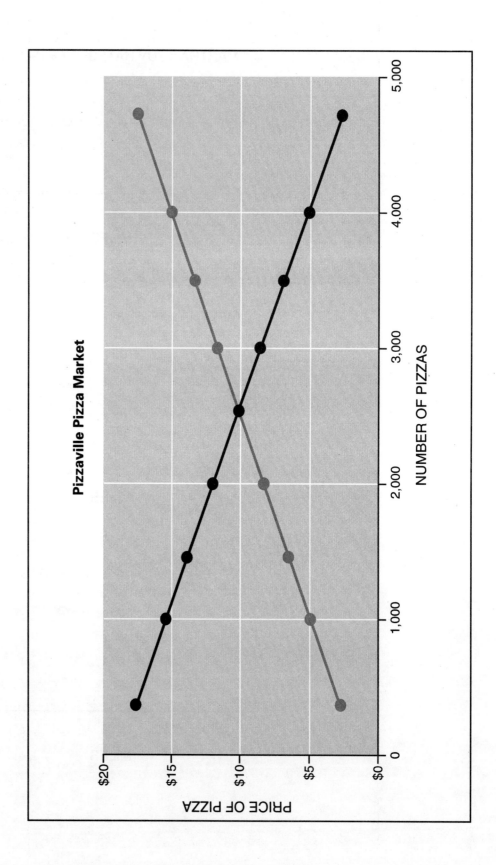

Change in Supply

1. At $10 for a large, two-topping pizza, two pizza makers from the neighboring town figure they can make good money selling pizzas in Pizzaville. To simplify things, we will say that the number of pizzas offered for sale will increase by exactly 1,000 pizzas at each price. Fill in the number of pizzas in Table A below for Supply 2 and plot the new supply line next to the original supply line. Label the new supply line "S2."

2. The equation for the original supply line is $y = 1/250x$. Find the equation for S2. S2 equation: $y = (1/250)(x) - 4$

3. Let's take another look at how the number of pizzas might increase as a result of new sellers entering the Pizzaville market. In this case, the number of pizzas increases by exactly 50% at each price. Fill in the number of pizzas in Table A for Supply 3. Plot the new supply line and label it S3. S3 equation: $y = (1/375)(x)$

Table A

Price of Pizza	Supply 1	Supply 2	Supply 3
$18	4,500	5,500	6,750
$16	4,000	5,000	6,000
$14	3,500	4,500	5,250
$12	3,000	4,000	4,500
$10	2,500	3,500	3,750
$ 8	2,000	3,000	3,000
$ 6	1,500	2,500	2,250
$ 4	1,000	2,000	1,500
$ 2	500	1,500	750

VISUAL 11.3 (continued)

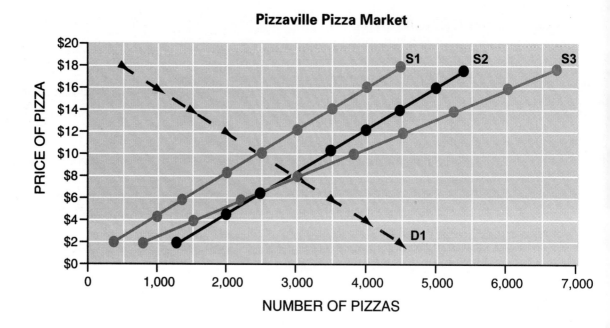

Pizzaville Pizza Market

4. In order to find the price of pizza in Pizzaville you will need to include the buyer's side of the market. Graph the demand line using the following ordered pairs: (4500, $2), (4000, $4), (3500, $6), (3000, $8), (2500, $10), (2000, $12), (1500, $14), (1000, $16), (500, $18). Using S1 and D1, the equilibrium price is $10 and the equilibrium number of pizzas is 2,500. Using S2 and D1, the equilibrium price is $8 and the equilibrium number of pizzas is 3,000. Using S3 and D1, the equilibrium price is $8 and the equilibrium number of pizzas is 3,000.

Compare and contrast S1, S2, S3. Complete the table below for the three supply lines. Put your answers in the appropriate boxes, then use the sections on the far right to make notes about the similarities and differences between the graphs in terms of their characteristics.

Characteristics	Items to be Compared			Compare and Contrast
	S1	S2	S3	
6. What is the slope of the line?	1/250	1/250	1/375	**Similarities** All positive **Differences** S3 changed
7. What is the y-intercept?	0	−4	0	**Similarities** S1 and S3 stayed the same **Differences** S2 changed
8. For S2 and S3, what words were used to indicate the amount of change in each supply line? What aspect of the equation changed?		Increased by 1,000 at each price y-intercept	Increased by 50% at each price slope	**Similarities** Changing some aspect of the number of pizzas changed both equations. **Differences** Adding 1,000 results in something different than multipling by 50%.
9. What change took place when the number of pizza sellers in Pizzaville increased?		Supply increased (More pizzas offered for sale.)	Supply increased (More pizzas offered for sale.)	**Similarities** Both changes increased the number of pizzas offered for sale. **Differences** Increased by different amounts.

10. How did increasing the number of sellers change the equilibrium price of pizza? (The equilibrium price decreased.)

11. Write a summary statement of what you have learned about the three supply lines in the Pizzaville pizza market.

VISUAL 11.4 ▲ Answers to Activity 11.2

Change in Demand

1. The city of Pizzaville decided to promote healthy eating for its residents by sponsoring a weight-loss program that offered awards to anyone who could lose ten pounds over the next three months. The effect of this program has caused some changes in the number of pizzas that people are willing to buy in Pizzaville. To keep things simple, we will say that the number of pizzas that people will buy will decrease by exactly 1,000 pizzas at each price. Fill in the number of pizzas in Table B below for Demand 2, and plot the new demand line next to the original demand line. Label the new demand "D2."

2. The equation for the original demand line is $y = 20 - (1/250)(x)$. Find the equation for D2. The D2 equation is: $y = (-1/250)(x) + 16$.

3. Let's take another look at how the number of pizzas might decrease as a result of people buying fewer pizzas. In this case, the number of pizzas decreases by exactly 75% at each price. Fill in the number of pizzas in Table B for Demand 3. Plot the new demand line and label it D3. D3 equation is: $y = (-2/125)(x) + 20$.

Table B

Price of Pizza	Demand 1	Demand 2	Demand 3
$18	500	−500	125
$16	1,000	0	250
$14	1,500	500	375
$12	2,000	1,000	500
$10	2,500	1,500	625
$ 8	3,000	2,000	750
$ 6	3,500	2,500	875
$ 4	4,000	3,000	1,000
$ 2	4,500	3,500	1,125

Pizzaville Pizza Market

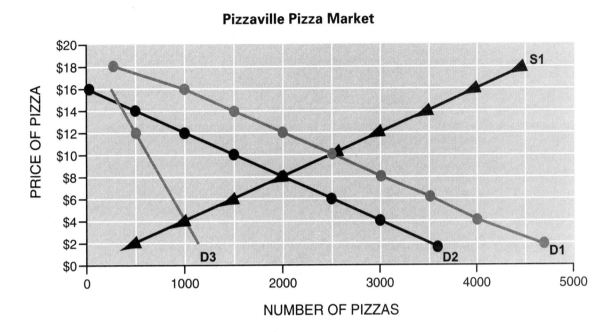

4. In order to find the price of pizza in Pizzaville you will need to include the seller's side of the market. Graph the supply line using the following ordered pairs: (500, $2), (1000, $4), (1500, $6), (2000, $8), (2500, $10), (3000, $12), (3500, $14), (4000, $16), (4500, $18). Using S1 and D1, the equilibrium price is $10 and the equilibrium number of pizzas is 2,500. Using S1 and D2, the equilibrium price is $8 and the equilibrium number of pizzas is 2,000. Using S1 and D3, the equilibrium price is $4 and the equilibrium number of pizzas is 1,000.

Compare and contrast D1, D2, D3. Complete questions 1-4 in the table below for the three supply lines from questions 4 and 5. Put your answers in the appropriate boxes; then use the sections on the far right to make notes about the similarities and differences between the graphs in terms of their characteristics.

Characteristics	Items to be Compared			Compare and Contrast
	D1	D2	D3	
5. What is the slope of the line?	−1/250	−1/250	−2/125	Similarities All negative Differences D3 changed.
6. What is the y-intercept?	20	16	20	Similarities All positive D3 stayed the same. Differences D2 changed.
7. For S2 and S3, what words were used to indicate the amount of change in each supply line? What aspect of the equation changed?		Decreased by exactly 1,000 pizzas at each price y-intercept	Decreased by 75% at each price slope	Similarities Changing some aspect of the number of pizzas changed both equations. Differences Subtracting 1,000 results in something different than decreasing by 75%.
8. What change took place when people were less willing to buy less pizza in order to lose weight?				Similarities Demand dropped for D2 and D3. Differences The decrease in pizzas people were willing to purchase differed between D2 and D3.

9. How did decreasing the number of pizzas people wanted to buy, change the equilibrium price of pizza? (It decreased.)

10. Write a summary statement of what you have learned about the three demand lines in the Pizzaville pizza market.

VISUAL 11.5

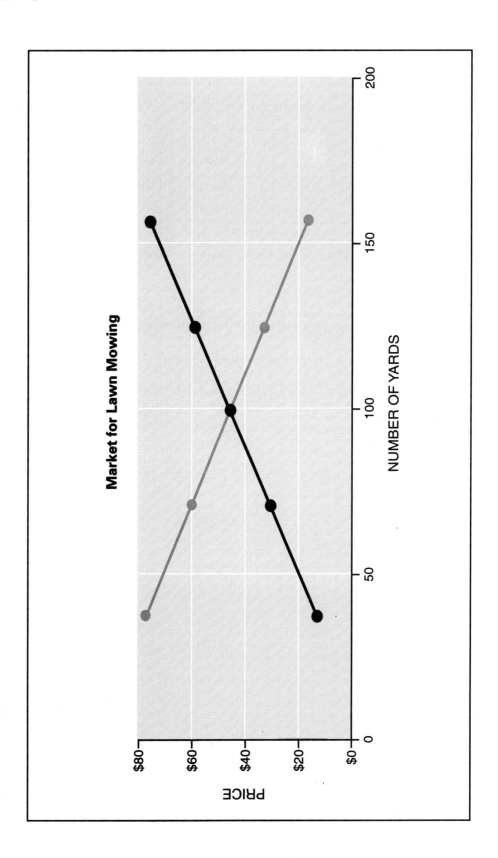

Price Change Cards: Front

Names: _____ and _____

Story Line:

Names: _____ and _____

Story Line:

Names: _____ and _____

Story Line:

Names: _____ and _____

Story Line:

Names: _____ and _____

Story Line:

Names: _____ and _____

Story Line:

Price Change Cards: Back

1. Fill in your names.

Names: _____ and _____

2. Does the story line represent a shift in

    Supply   or   Demand

3. Make a prediction about the change
in price either up or down.

Price Prediction: _____

---

1. Fill in your names.

Names: _____ and _____

2. Does the story line represent a shift in

    Supply   or   Demand

3. Make a prediction about the change
in price either up or down.

Price Prediction: _____

---

1. Fill in your names.

Names: _____ and _____

2. Does the story line represent a shift in

    Supply   or   Demand

3. Make a prediction about the change
in price either up or down.

Price Prediction: _____

---

1. Fill in your names.

Names: _____ and _____

2. Does the story line represent a shift in

    Supply   or   Demand

3. Make a prediction about the change
in price either up or down.

Price Prediction: _____

---

1. Fill in your names.

Names: _____ and _____

2. Does the story line represent a shift in

    Supply   or   Demand

3. Make a prediction about the change
in price either up or down.

Price Prediction: _____

---

1. Fill in your names.

Names: _____ and _____

2. Does the story line represent a shift in

    Supply   or   Demand

3. Make a prediction about the change
in price either up or down.

Price Prediction: _____

Charting a Budget

Mathematics Prerequisites

Prior to this lesson, students should know:
➤ How to add integers.
➤ How to convert among rational number forms.
➤ How to find a percent of a number.
➤ How to construct a pie chart.

Lesson Objectives

Students will be able to:
➤ Define *budget, surplus, deficit*, and *taxes*.
➤ Explain that individuals and governments have budgets.
➤ Compare expected income with expected revenue to determine whether a deficit, a surplus or a balance is likely to occur.
➤ Explain that governments pay for the goods and services they use or provide by taxing people.
➤ Explain that most federal tax revenue comes from personal income and payroll taxes.
➤ Identify various expenses for the federal government.

Abstract

In this lesson, students learn what a budget is. They construct a pie chart to show the distribution of expenses in a budget. They learn about payroll deductions and determine the impact that payroll deductions have on a budget. Finally, they learn that the U.S. federal government uses tax revenue to pay for the goods and services it uses and provides. They construct graphs that represent the federal government's budget of projected income and expenses for 2002.

Mathematics Terms

➤ Rational number forms, fractions, decimals and percents
➤ Percents
➤ Circle graph

Materials

➤ One copy of Activities 12.1–12.5 for each student
➤ Transparencies of Visuals 12.1–12.7
➤ Protractor for each student

Estimated Time

Two to three class periods

Warm-Up Activities

1. Ask the students how many colors are in an M&M's® package. (Six: brown, red, yellow, orange, green, blue.)

2. Point out that when M&M's® produces 20 M&M candies for regular distribution, it includes the following amounts of each color.
   - 6 brown
   - 2 orange
   - 4 red
   - 2 green
   - 4 yellow
   - 2 blue

3. Assign the following.
   - Write each color as a ratio. (6/20, 4/20, 4/20, 2/20, 2/20, 2/20)
   - Change each ratio to a decimal. (.3, .2, .2, .1, .1, .1)
   - Change each decimal to a percent. (30%, 20%, 20%, 10%, 10%, 10%)
   - Find the number of degrees for each color. (108, 72, 72, 36, 36, 36)
   - Make a pie chart of the colors. (See Visual 12.1 for correct answer.)

4. Tell the students that the Mars candy company manufactures approximately 300 million pieces of M&M's® every day. Assign the following.
   - Write this number in standard form and with a decimal point in hundred millions. (300,000,000; 3.00 hundred million)
   - Given this information, how many M&M's® would be produced in one, five-day workweek? *(Write this number in standard form and as a decimal number in billions.)* (1,5000,000,000; 1.5 billion)
   - How many would be produced in 52 weeks*? (Write in standard form and in billions.)* (78,000,000,000; 52 x 1.5 billion = 78 billion)

Procedure

1. Ask the students if they have done jobs and earned income, and ask how they earned it. (Babysitting, lawn mowing, allowance for doing household chores, raking leaves)

2. Remind them that they will soon be old enough to earn income by working at stores, restaurants, movie theatres, and other businesses in the community. Explain that many people manage their income by making a budget. Define *budget* as a financial plan that summarizes future income and expenditures over a period of time. People use budgets to consider carefully how they will spend their income. Read the following scenario to the class.

   Ang Lee will turn 16 on his birthday next month. Ang is very excited that he'll now be able to drive. His parents gave him permission to *drive the family car. What freedom! His parents told him that he must pay for his car insurance—$1200 a year. He must also pay for the gas that he uses. He's also responsible for other personal expenditures, such as movies, snacks, and CDs. His parents told him that he should make a budget to see if he can earn enough money to pay for all the things he needs. Ang doesn't expect any problems. He knows that he can get a part-time job and be very careful with his money. After all, he's very sensible!*

Ang found a job bagging groceries eight hours on Saturday and four hours on Sunday afternoon at the local grocery store for $7.00 an hour. He'd earn $336 a month–more than enough! Ang took the job, began to work on his budget, and studied for his driver's test. Life was good!

3. Display Visual 12.2 and ask the following.
   a. What are the major categories in Ang's budget? (Income, expenses, and surplus/deficit.)
   b. How did Ang determine that he would earn $336 a month? (12 hours x $7 x 4 weekends)
   c. How did Ang plan to spend his income? (Car insurance, gasoline, going out, and other items such as clothes and CDs.)
   d. Ang projected that he would have a surplus of $21.00 every month. What is a surplus? (Students are likely to answer "extra." Guide them to define a surplus as a positive amount of income remaining after expenses.) Have the students write a math sentence for a surplus. [Surplus = (income > expenses)].

4. Give a copy of Activities 12.1 and 12.2 to each student and assign. When the students have finished, point out that data can be represented in many ways. (Answers to Activity 12.1 appear on Visual 12.3 and answers to Activity 12.2 appear on Visual 12.4.) Ask the following.
   a. How much income did Ang estimate he would spend? ($336)
   b. Name the ways his expense and surplus data were represented. (1. dollar amounts; 2. decimal amounts; 3. percentages; 4. degrees; and 5. pictorially, as a circle graph/pie chart.)
   c. Which representation makes it easiest for you to get an idea of how Ang spends his income? (Answers will vary, but students tend to answer that the pie chart is easiest. With this example, few numbers are presented, so students may find the dollar amount easily.)

5. Tell the students that Ang received his first paycheck and came home in shock. Ang had not considered that his paycheck would have payroll deductions. Display Visual 12.5 and ask the students to identify the different taxes that Ang must pay on his income. (Federal and state income taxes and FICA.) Explain that FICA (Federal Insurance Contributions Act) is a payroll tax that pays for Social Security and Medicare contributions.

6. Explain that Ang now has a deficit in his budget. Point out that, in many cases for financial data, negative numbers are displayed with parentheses. Ang is spending more than he earns. Have the students write a math sentence to describe a deficit. [Deficit = (Income < Expenses)]. Ask the students the following:

   a. How could Ang continue with a deficit month after month? (He couldn't, unless he borrowed money every month or used some past savings.)

   b. What could Ang do to eliminate his deficit? (He could increase his income or reduce his expenses.)

7. Explain that the students will now learn why governments collect taxes. Give a copy of Activity 12.3 to each student and assign. When the students have completed the work, ask the following questions:

   a. What percent of his income is deducted for federal income taxes? (15%)

   b. What percent of his income is deducted for state income taxes? (6%) Point out that not all states have an income tax and, for those that do, the rates vary from state to state.

   c. What percent of his income is deducted for Social Security and Medicare? (7.65%)

   d. What percent of his income does he take home? (71.35%)

8. Explain that Ang was upset to learn that state and federal governments kept money that he had earned. He asked his parents to explain why this was happening. " After all," Ang said, "Why do the governments need money? They don't do anything for anybody." Ang's parents suggested that Ang do some research to find out what happens to the tax revenue governments collect.

9. Give a copy of Activity 12.4 to each student, explaining that *taxes* are required payments to government. Point out the four major sources of revenue for the federal government: individual income taxes, social insurance receipts (e.g., Social Security and Medicare), corporate income taxes, and other taxes, such as excise taxes and customs duties. (Answers to Activity 12.4 appear on Visual 12.6.)

10. Initiate a discussion on what the students think the federal government spends its money on and where it spends the most money. Accept a wide variety of answers. Give a copy of Activity 12.5 to each student, explaining that this worksheet examines how the government planned to spend its money in 2002. Explain the spending items as follows.

    ➤ Social Security refers to income assistance to older people, children who have lost an income-earning parent, and people who have become disabled. It is an insurance program, and payments are only made to people (or their dependents) who have paid into the program.

➤ The government provides much health-care assistance in the forms of Medicare and Medicaid in addition to other health-care programs.

➤ National defense refers primarily to military expenses.

➤ Income security refers to programs, other than Social Security, Medicare, and Medicaid, where the federal government gives money to help people, such as welfare programs.

➤ Net interest refers primarily to the interest payments on the national debt. For many years, the federal government ran a deficit—it spent more than it received. As a result, the government had to borrow money from the public. Individuals and businesses own government securities, such as savings bonds. These are loans to the government, and the individuals and businesses receive interest from the government for the use of their money. Make sure that the students do not equate a budget deficit with the national debt. A deficit occurs in one fiscal year. The national debt is the accumulated amount of money owed to individuals and businesses.

➤ "Other expenses" is a broad category. It includes spending on natural resources and the environment, energy, education, agriculture, transportation, and a wide variety of other programs that are not included in the other categories.

11. Discuss the following, based on Activity 12.5. (Answers to Activity 12.5 appear on Visual 12.7.)

a. What is the largest expense for the federal government? (Social Security payments.)

b. What is the next highest expense for the federal government? (Health programs and Medicare.)

c. What is the smallest expense category shown? (Net interest.) Point out that this expense category was a much higher percentage in other years when the federal government had to pay higher interest rates to its borrowers. Interest rates were projected to be relatively low in 2002.

d. In July 2001, did the government project a budget surplus or deficit? (Surplus.) How much? ($231 billion.)

e. If Ang reduced his expenditures or worked more so that he had a budget surplus projected, what could he do with the surplus? (Save it.) Point out that saving some income can help with a person's unexpected expenses. If Ang had a car accident, he would have to pay some part of the repairs, even if he has car insurance.

f. If the federal government ran a surplus in its budget, what could it do with the money? (Give the taxpayers a tax rebate, pay off some of the national debt.)

12. Summarize the main points of the lesson with the following.

   ➤ A budget is a financial plan that summarizes future income and expenditures over a period of time.

   ➤ If the projected income exceeds the expenses, a surplus exists. If the projected income is less than the expenses, a deficit exists.

   ➤ Paychecks usually have payroll deductions such as federal income taxes, state income taxes, and FICA (Social Security and Medicare).

   ➤ Taxes are required payments to governments.

   ➤ Governments use tax revenues and other receipts to pay for their expenses.

   ➤ The largest expense items in the federal budget tend to be Social Security, health programs and Medicare, and national defense.

   ➤ Fractions, decimals and percents can be used as different forms of the same number to help solve problems.

   ➤ Percents can be converted to degrees of a circle so that pie charts can be drawn.

   ➤ Finding the percent of a number helps us to understand how a part relates to a whole.

ACTIVITY 12.1 ▲ Budget Table

The table below shows Ang Lee's estimated expenses. He will earn an estimated monthly income of $336. Using the procedure in the example, complete the table. Use the information in columns 4 and 5 to construct a circle graph (pie chart) in Activity 12.2.

Example: car insurance

Column 3: To calculate the portion of income spent for car insurance, divide $100 (figure in column 2) by $336. (Round to two decimal places.)

Column 4: To convert .30 from a decimal to a percent, multiply by 100.

Column 5: To calculate the portion of a circle (degrees) represented by the car insurance expense, multiply .30 (figure in column 3) by 360. Round to the nearest whole number.

1 Item	2 $ Amount	3 $ Amount 336	4 %	5 Degrees
Car insurance	100.00	.30	30%	108°
Gas	60.00			
Going out	80.00			
Clothes, CDs	75.00			
Surplus	21.00			

ACTIVITY 12.2 ▲ Budget Circle

Using the information from Activity 12.1 and a protractor, construct a circle graph (pie chart).

Step 1: Place the center of the protractor on the center of the circle, making sure the bottom of the protractor is on the line.

Step 2: Measure and mark 108° on the circumference. Draw a radius from the center point to the 108° mark.

Step 3: Label this segment *car insurance 30%*.

Step 4: For the next item, draw a new radius the correct number of degrees beyond the 108° mark for the gas expense. Label the segment.

Step 5: Repeat this process for all expenses and the surplus.

Step 6: Color each segment a different color.

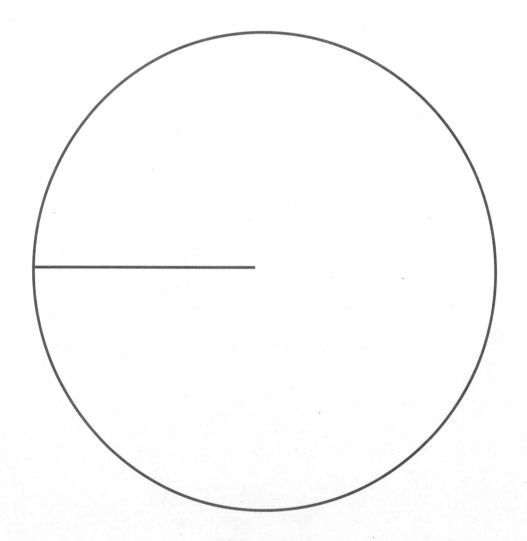

ACTIVITY 12.3 ▲ Dividing Up the Money

Income taxes and payroll taxes (Social Security and Medicare) are deducted from employees' paychecks. Ang Lee earned $336 a month. He paid $50.40 in federal income taxes, $20.16 in state income taxes, and $25.70 in payroll taxes (FICA), leaving $239.74 as take-home pay.

1. Calculate the percent of Ang's income for each deduction.

   Federal income tax   _____%

   State income tax   _____%

   FICA   _____%

2. Think of the dollar bill below as a stacked bar graph. Draw vertical lines to divide the dollar bill into segments representing Ang's federal income taxes, state income taxes, FICA, and take-home pay. Label each segment with the item and percent. Below the dollar bill, write a title for the graph. (Hint: Divide the bottom of the dollar into tenths, each tenth representing 10 cents.)

_____

ACTIVITY 12.4 ▲ Where the Federal Government Dollar Comes From

☆☆☆ The Federal Budget 2002: Part I ☆☆☆
$ $ $ Sources of Revenue $ $ $

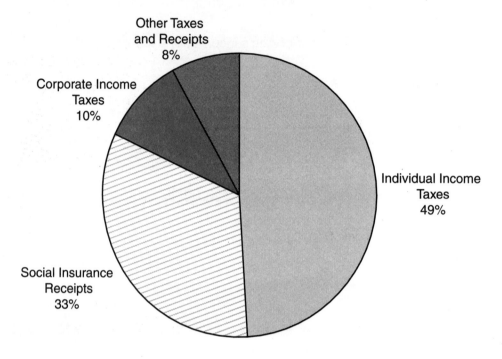

Source: Office of Management and Budget, July 2001.

Early in the George W. Bush administration, the Office of Management and Budget (OMB) estimated a federal budget for 2002. The projected revenue was $2.192 trillion.

1. Write the full number in standard form for $2.192 trillion.

   _____

2. Determine the dollar amount for the following.

   a. Individual income taxes   _____

   b. Social insurance receipts   _____

   c. Corporate income taxes   _____

   d. Other taxes and receipts   _____

ACTIVITY 12.5 ▲ How Your Tax Dollar Is Used

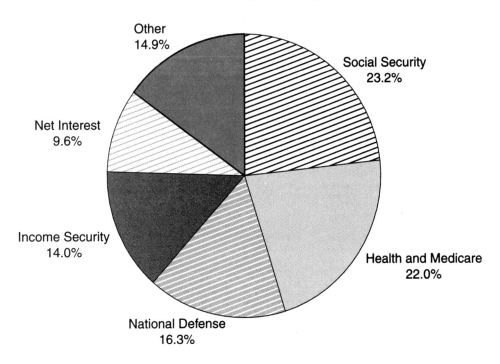

☆☆☆ The Federal Budget 2002: Part II ☆☆☆
$ $ $ Federal Spending $ $ $

In July 2001, the OMB also estimated the federal government's spending for 2002. The budget indicated that federal spending would be $1.961 trillion.

How much would the federal government spend on the following?

1. Social Security   _____

2. Medicare and health   _____

3. National defense   _____

4. Income security   _____

5. Net interest   _____

6. Other spending   _____

In 2002, the Bush administration projects a: *surplus* *deficit* (circle one) that amounts to

$_____.

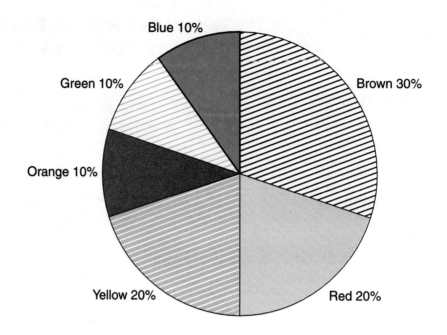

Blue 10%

Green 10%

Brown 30%

Orange 10%

Yellow 20%

Red 20%

VISUAL 12.2 ▲ Ang's Monthly Budget

Item	$
Income	336.00
Expenses	
Car insurance	100.00
Gas	60.00
Going out	80.00
Clothes, CDs	75.00
Surplus (Deficit)	21.00

Budget Table

The table below shows Ang Lee's estimated expenses. He will earn an estimated monthly income of $336. Using the procedure in the example, complete the table. Use the information in columns 4 and 5 to construct a circle graph (pie chart) in Activity 12.2.

Example: car insurance

Column 3: To calculate the portion of income spent for car insurance, divide $100 (figure in column 2) by $336. (Round to two decimal places.)

Column 4: To convert .30 from a decimal to a percent, multiply by 100.

Column 5: To calculate the portion of a circle (degrees) represented by the car insurance expense, multiply .30 (figure in column 3) by 360. Round to the nearest whole number.

| 1 | 2 | 3 | 4 | 5 |
| | | $ Amount | | |
Item	$ Amount	336	%	Degrees
Car insurance	100.00	.30	30%	108°
Gas	60.00	.18	18%	65°
Going out	80.00	.24	24%	86°
Clothes, CDs	75.00	.22	22%	79°
Surplus	21.00	.06	6%	22°

Budget Circle

Ang Lee's Estimated Expenses

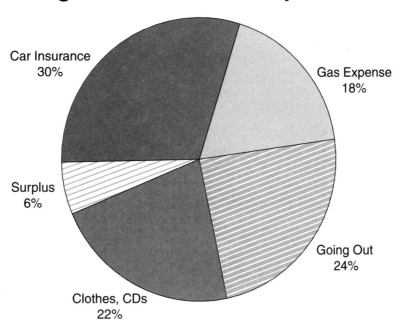

VISUAL 12.5 ▲ Ang's Angst

Item	$
Income	336.00
Federal income taxes	50.40
State income taxes	20.16
FICA	25.70
Take-Home Pay	239.74
Expenses	
Car Insurance	100.00
Gas	60.00
Going Out	80.00
Clothes, CDs	75.00
Surplus (Deficit)	(75.26)

☆☆☆ The Federal Budget 2002: Part I ☆☆☆
$ $ $ Sources of Revenue $ $ $

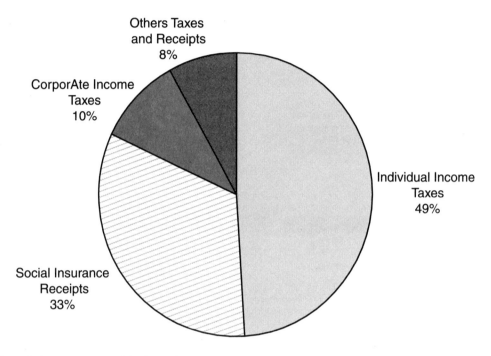

Source: Office of Management and Budget, July 2001.

Early in the George W. Bush administration, the Office of Management and Budget (OMB) estimated a federal budget for 2002. The projected revenue was $2.192 trillion.

1. Write the full number in standard form for $2.192 trillion. ($2,192,000,000,000)

2. Determine the dollar amount for the following.

    a. Individual income taxes   ($1.074 trillion)

    b. Social insurance receipts   ($723.36 billion)

    c. Corporate income taxes   ($219.2 billion)

    d. Other taxes and receipts   ($175.36 billion)

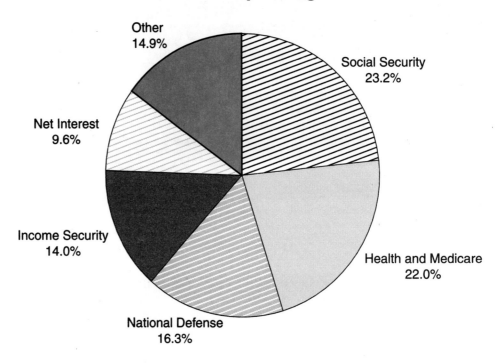

☆☆☆ The Federal Budget 2002: Part II ☆☆☆
$ $ $ Federal Spending $ $ $

Other 14.9%

Social Security 23.2%

Net Interest 9.6%

Income Security 14.0%

Health and Medicare 22.0%

National Defense 16.3%

In July 2001, the OMB also estimated the federal government's spending for 2002. The budget indicated that federal spending would be $1.961 trillion.

How much would the federal government spend on the following?

1. Social Security   ($455.0 billion)

2. Medicare and health   ($431.4 billion)

3. National defense   ($319.6 billion)

4. Income security   ($274.5 billion)

5. Net interest   ($188.3 billion)

6. Other spending   ($292.2 billion)

In 2002, the Bush administration projects a   *surplus*   *deficit*   (circle one) that amounts to $ ($231 billion).

Notes

Notes

Notes

Notes

Notes

Notes